An Analysis of

Clifford Geertz's

The Interpretation of Cultures

Selected Essays

T0301892

Abena Dadze-Arthur

Published by Macat International Ltd
24:13 Coda Centre, 189 Munster Road, London SW6 6AW.

Distributed exclusively by Routledge
2 Park Square, Milton Park, Abingdon, Oxon OX14 4RN
711 Third Avenue, New York, NY 10017, USA

Routledge is an imprint of the Taylor & Francis Group, an informa business

www.macat.com
info@macat.com

Cataloguing in Publication Data
A catalogue record for this book is available from the British Library.
Library of Congress Cataloguing-in-Publication Data is available upon request.
Cover illustration: Capucine Deslouis

ISBN 978-1-912302-06-2 (hardback)
ISBN 978-1-912127-28-3 (paperback)
ISBN 978-1-912128-31-0 (e-book)

CONTENTS

THE MACAT LIBRARY

The Macat Library is a series of unique academic explorations of seminal works in the humanities and social sciences – books and papers that have had a significant and widely recognised impact on their disciplines. It has been created to serve as much more than just a summary of what lies between the covers of a great book. It illuminates and explores the influences on, ideas of, and impact of that book. Our goal is to offer a learning resource that encourages critical thinking and fosters a better, deeper understanding of important ideas.

Each publication is divided into three Sections: Influences, Ideas, and Impact. Each Section has four Modules. These explore every important facet of the work, and the responses to it.

This Section-Module structure makes a Macat Library book easy to use, but it has another important feature. Because each Macat book is written to the same format, it is possible (and encouraged!) to cross-reference multiple Macat books along the same lines of inquiry or research. This allows the reader to open up interesting interdisciplinary pathways.

To further aid your reading, lists of glossary terms and people mentioned are included at the end of this book (these are indicated by an asterisk [*] throughout) – as well as a list of works cited.

Macat has worked with the University of Cambridge to identify the elements of critical thinking and understand the ways in which six different skills combine to enable effective thinking.
Three allow us to fully understand a problem; three more give us the tools to solve it. Together, these six skills make up the **PACIER** model of critical thinking. They are:

ANALYSIS – understanding how an argument is built
EVALUATION – exploring the strengths and weaknesses of an argument
INTERPRETATION – understanding issues of meaning

CREATIVE THINKING – coming up with new ideas and fresh connections
PROBLEM-SOLVING – producing strong solutions
REASONING – creating strong arguments

To find out more, visit **WWW.MACAT.COM.**

CRITICAL THINKING AND *THE INTERPRETATION OF CULTURES*

Primary critical thinking skill: INTERPRETATION
Secondary critical thinking skill: CREATIVE THINKING

Clifford Geertz has been called 'the most original anthropologist of his generation' – and this reputation rests largely on the huge contributions to the methodology and approaches of anthropological interpretation that he outlined in *The Interpretation of Cultures*.

The centrality of interpretative skills to anthropology is uncontested: in a subject that is all about understanding mankind, and which seeks to outline the differences and the common ground that exists between cultures, interpretation is the crucial skillset. For Geertz, however, standard interpretative approaches did not go deep enough, and his life's work concentrated on deepening and perfecting his subject's interpretative skills.

Geertz is best known for his definition of 'culture,' and his theory of 'thick description,' an influential technique that depends on fresh interpretative approaches. For Geertz, 'cultures' are 'webs of meaning' in which everyone is suspended. Understanding culture, therefore, is not so much a matter of going in search of law, but of setting out an interpretative framework for meaning that focuses directly on attempts to define the real meaning of things within a given culture. The best way to do this, for Geertz, is via 'thick description:' a way of recording things that explores context and surroundings, and articulates meaning within the web of culture. Ambitious and bold, Geertz's greatest creation is a method all critical thinkers can learn from.

ABOUT THE AUTHOR OF THE ORIGINAL WORK

Born in San Francisco in 1926, American anthropologist **Clifford Geertz** was raised in a foster family in rural California after his parents divorced. Completing two years of military service during World War II, he went on to earn a PhD in anthropology from Harvard.

Harvard's newly formed Department of Social Relations took an interdisciplinary approach to anthropology, and this idea, which was novel at the time, shaped Geertz's work throughout his long academic career. That career included 30 years as professor of social science at Princeton University's Institute of Advanced Study, but Geertz was also a prolific field researcher and author. A 'major intellectual figure of the twentieth century' – as one colleague called him – Geertz died in 2006.

ABOUT THE AUTHOR OF THE ANALYSIS

Dr Abena Dadze-Arthur holds an MSc in contemporary political sociology from the London School of Economics and a doctorate in culturally-rooted public management from the University of Birmingham. She is currently a lecturer in the School of Government and Society at Birmingham.

ABOUT MACAT

GREAT WORKS FOR CRITICAL THINKING

Macat is focused on making the ideas of the world's great thinkers accessible and comprehensible to everybody, everywhere, in ways that promote the development of enhanced critical thinking skills.

It works with leading academics from the world's top universities to produce new analyses that focus on the ideas and the impact of the most influential works ever written across a wide variety of academic disciplines. Each of the works that sit at the heart of its growing library is an enduring example of great thinking. But by setting them in context – and looking at the influences that shaped their authors, as well as the responses they provoked – Macat encourages readers to look at these classics and game-changers with fresh eyes. Readers learn to think, engage and challenge their ideas, rather than simply accepting them.

"Macat offers an amazing first-of-its-kind tool for interdisciplinary learning and research. Its focus on works that transformed their disciplines and its rigorous approach, drawing on the world's leading experts and educational institutions, opens up a world-class education to anyone."

Andreas Schleicher
Director for Education and Skills, Organisation for Economic
Co-operation and Development

'Macat is taking on some of the major challenges in university education … They have drawn together a strong team of active academics who are producing teaching materials that are novel in the breadth of their approach.'

Prof Lord Broers,
former Vice-Chancellor of the University of Cambridge

'The Macat vision is exceptionally exciting. It focuses upon new modes of learning which analyse and explain seminal texts which have profoundly influenced world thinking and so social and economic development. It promotes the kind of critical thinking which is essential for any society and economy.
This is the learning of the future.'

Rt Hon Charles Clarke, former UK Secretary of State for Education

'The Macat analyses provide immediate access to the critical conversation surrounding the books that have shaped their respective discipline, which will make them an invaluable resource to all of those, students and teachers, working in the field.'

Professor William Tronzo, University of California at San Diego

WAYS IN TO THE TEXT

KEY POINTS

- The American cultural anthropologist* Clifford Geertz conducted extensive field research in the Pacific nation of Indonesia,* which inspired the essays in his 1973 publication *The Interpretation of Cultures.* Geertz died in 2006.

- Cultural anthropology looks at the variations among human cultures. Many considered Geertz the most important cultural anthropologist in the United States.

- Geertz defined culture* as a system of shared meaning that ought to be studied by interpreting the symbols of that culture, such as art and myths. *The Interpretation of Cultures* came to define the field. Although the general public often misunderstood the book, it remains one of the most cited works among academics across disciplines.

Who Was Clifford Geertz?

The cultural anthropologist Clifford Geertz is best known for his 1973 work *The Interpretation of Cultures*. He was born on August 23, 1926 in San Francisco in the United States. Geertz was only three years old when his father and mother split up. He was then taken in by foster parents who lived in a rural part of California. At the age of 17, Geertz signed up with the US Navy. Following two years of military service, Geertz left the Navy at the end of World War II* in 1945.

After the war, Geertz went to study at Antioch College in Ohio with funding from the GI Bill (money granted by the government to veterans of World War II), and graduated in 1950 with a degree in philosophy. He moved on to graduate school at the prestigious Harvard University, studying with two famous scholars: Clyde Kluckhohn,* a professor of anthropology, and Talcott Parsons,* a professor of sociology.* Geertz obtained his doctorate in anthropology in 1956.

In the 15 years that followed, Geertz produced the essays eventually collected in *The Interpretation of Cultures*. These essays evolved from insights he gained from field research in Bali, Java, and Sumatra, three islands in the Indonesian archipelago. He conducted his research there with his first wife, Hildred Storey Geertz,* also a famous anthropologist.

In 1970 Geertz became a professor of social science at the Institute for Advanced Study in Princeton, New Jersey, where he worked for 30 years until the end of his career. Clifford and Hildred had no children and divorced after 32 years. Geertz later married Karen Blu,* another anthropologist, and they had two children together.

Geertz never recovered from heart surgery and died on October 30, 2006. The cultural anthropologist Richard Allan Shweder,* who studied with Geertz, described him as "an unpretentious, even somewhat introverted man, who was skittish and halting yet also riveting and dazzling in interpersonal encounters."[1]

What Does *The Interpretation of Cultures* Say?

The Interpretation of Cultures, published in 1973, set out "a treatise in cultural theory."[2] The book formally and systematically explains what culture is and how we ought to study it. It helped redefine the discipline of anthropology. It also influenced the emergence of cultural anthropology, which studies the cultural variations between different peoples and societies, as well as how people behave, communicate, and socialize with one another.

Geertz defined culture as "a system of inherited conceptions expressed in symbolic forms."[3] In other words, he viewed culture as an organized collection of symbols and signs that carry particular meaning. For example, the statue of the dying Jesus on a cross is a symbol that carries a religious meaning and forms part of a cultural system called religion. Even people who are not religious and therefore outsiders to this particular cultural system recognize the symbol.

Based on his concept of culture, Geertz believed we ought to study it in a particular way. In *The Interpretation of Cultures*, he offered two key ideas about how to do that.

First, he suggested that anthropologists can only understand culture properly if they look at how people express themselves through symbols, signs, symbolic acts, and rituals. For example, for Christians, eating bread and drinking wine during a Church service is a symbolic act. It represents eating the flesh and drinking the blood of Christ. The members of this culture, then, use these symbolic acts to celebrate the love of their God that transforms death into new life.

Second, Geertz says anthropologists ought to study culture from the perspective of the people concerned. He believes that "cultures and peoples should speak for themselves, with anthropologists learning to converse with them and interpret them."[4] In other words, culture ought to be interpreted from the viewpoint of the person whose culture it actually is.

This means that anthropologists should read the meanings of symbols or symbolic acts just as native people do, and then translate and convey their meanings to outsiders. Geertz calls this process an interpretive approach.* Interpretive scholars must explain and clarify the realities that different groups of people have built in their social world.

Of course, all interpretations must necessarily be rooted in a particular moment. They apply to a specific time, context, and situation. Having said that, conversations can cause interpretations to be revised and renegotiated to a certain extent. Because of this, the interpretivist approach Geertz lays out suggests researchers can only produce adequate interpretations if they view the world through the eyes of the people they seek to understand.

Why Does *The Interpretation of Cultures Matter*?

The Interpretation of Cultures established Geertz as "a major voice" of the "symbolic" or interpretive anthropology movement of the 1960s.[5] For many people, both inside and outside of the discipline, *The Interpretation of Cultures* explained not only what Geertz did, but also what cultural anthropologists in general do.[6]

The Interpretation of Cultures also influenced how cultural anthropology is done today. Geertz said that nurturing a dialogue between researcher and subject is crucial. Doing this requires carefully observing and interviewing people about the meanings of their symbols and symbolic actions. Working this way gives anthropologists a more informed and sophisticated understanding of what they examine. It also enables them to see better how people understand themselves, others, and the world around them. Such an understanding in turn helps anthropologists develop more comprehensive and representative interpretations of societies.

The Interpretation of Cultures shows us a way to understand different ways of life.[7] Given the world's ever increasing cultural, moral, scientific, and political diversity, understanding our differences remains as relevant and timely today as it was when Geertz was working in the 1960s. As the influential cultural anthropologist Sherry Ortner* argues, Geertz's book has a "timeless quality" and is useful for everyone.[8]

The Interpretation of Cultures was among the most cited works in the 2007 *Handbook on Cultural Psychology*.[9] The *New York Times Literary Supplement* called it "one of the 100 most important books since World War II."[10] It remains essential reading for anyone who wants to interpret the meanings of people's actions in the world.[11]

NOTES

1 Richard Shweder, *Clifford James Geertz: 1926–2006, A Biographical Memoir* (Washington, DC: National Academy of Sciences), 5, accessed November 2, 2015, https:/www.sss.ias.edu/files/pdfs/Geertz_NAS_6–10-10.pdf.

2 Clifford Geertz, *The Interpretation of Cultures*, 2nd edn (New York: Basic Books, 2000), viii.

3 Geertz, *The Interpretation of Cultures*, 89.

4 Andrew Yarrow, "Clifford Geertz, Cultural Anthropologist, Is Dead at 80," *New York Times*, November 1, 2006, accessed December 8, 2015, http:/www.nytimes.com/2006/11/01/obituaries/01geertz.html?pagewanted=print&_r=0.

5 Richard Shweder, "The Resolute Irresolution of Clifford Geertz," *Common Knowledge* 13, nos. 2–3 (Spring–Fall 2007): 191–205.

6 Richard Shweder and Byron Good, eds., *Clifford Geertz by His Colleagues* (Chicago: University of Chicago Press, 2005).

7 Shweder, "The Resolute Irresolution of Clifford Geertz," 203.

8 Sherry Ortner, "Special Issue: The Fate of 'Culture': Geertz and beyond," *Representations* 59 (1997): 7.

9 Shweder, "The Resolute Irresolution of Clifford Geertz," 203.

10 Yarrow, "Clifford Geertz."

11 See Ortner, "Special Issue," 7.

SECTION 1
INFLUENCES

MODULE 1
THE AUTHOR AND THE HISTORICAL CONTEXT

KEY POINTS

- Scholars consider *The Interpretation of Cultures* one of the founding texts of interpretive anthropology* (an approach to anthropological research that proposes that peoples and cultures should represent themselves, and that anthropologists should learn to interpret cultural meanings to outsiders).

- A range of academic disciplines influenced Geertz's work, evidenced by his lifelong passion for interdisciplinary* experimentation; "interdisciplinary" refers to research that draws on the aims and methods of different academic disciplines.

- By the 1960s, the field of anthropology sought to distance itself from its colonial* origins (its origins in the period of European political and economic exploitation of foreign territories and people, particularly in the nineteenth century) and reinvent itself as an area of study that explores the ways people see themselves and their world.

Why Read This Text?

Arguing for the need to embrace an interpretive approach to the field of anthropology, Clifford Geertz's *The Interpretation of Cultures* (1973) remains essential reading for students of this discipline.

In it, Geertz proposes that interpretive anthropology has two purposes: first, to see the world through the eyes of those born into a given culture; second, to translate the resulting insight to those outside the culture—an approach known as interpretivism.

f Let me instead take the rather peculiar tack of thanking three remarkable academic institutions that have provided me with the kind of setting for scholarly work I am convinced could not be surpassed right now anywhere in the world: The Department of Social Relations of Harvard University, where I was trained; the Department of Anthropology of the University of Chicago, where I taught for a decade; and The Institute for Advanced Study in Princeton, where I now work. "

Clifford Geertz, *The Interpretation of Cultures*

The interpretive approach to studying culture revolutionized the field of anthropology. Geertz was among the first generation of scholars to propose that outsiders should study culture by understanding the subjective perspectives of those living in the culture (that is, the world as it was understood by people from other cultures). Until then, practitioners had believed that anthropologists should study a culture "objectively from the outside" as detached observers.[1] Aram Yengoyan,* a well-respected social anthropologist* (a scholar of social structures and their role in human cultures) with particular expertise in southeast Asia, has argued that *The Interpretation of Cultures* offered a new form of anthropology. Geertz's approach differed significantly from the anthropology advocated by his contemporaries.[2]

The Interpretation of Cultures also made an impact beyond the confines of anthropology, influencing disciplines in the social sciences and humanities. The academic world recognized the importance of *The Interpretation of Cultures* immediately following its publication in 1973. Only a year later, the volume won the 1974 Sorokin Award of the American Sociological Association. When the work was republished in 2000, *The New York Times* celebrated it as "one of the 100 most important books since World War II."*[3] But the general public never fully appreciated the importance of Geertz's book.

Author's Life
Clifford Geertz was born in 1926 in San Francisco, a city in the US state of California. His parents separated when Geertz was three years old, and sent him to rural California to be brought up by foster parents. When Geertz turned 17, he enlisted with the US Navy. He served in World War II from 1943 until 1945.

Following his naval service, Geertz studied philosophy at Antioch College in Ohio, where the philosopher George Geiger* mentored him. After graduating in 1950, Geertz applied for a PhD at Harvard University's newly founded interdisciplinary Department of Social Relations.[4] Two famous American scholars led this department: the sociologist* Talcott Parsons* and the cultural anthropologist* Clyde Kluckhohn;* sociology is the study of the nature and history of human society, while cultural anthropology is the study of human beliefs and practices as they are understood to constitute "culture." Geertz later reported that the unique academic culture of the new department at Harvard infected him with "a great excitement about interdisciplinary experimentation."[5] This would become a lifelong characteristic and integral part of his work.

In 1960, Geertz joined the Anthropology Department at the distinguished University of Chicago. During his decade in Chicago, Geertz championed his particular concept of culture.[6] In 1970, he moved to Princeton University, becoming a professor of social science at the Institute for Advanced Study. He stayed there for the rest of his career, becoming a professor emeritus in 2000. In Princeton, Geertz established himself as what Peter Goddard, director of the institute, described as a "major intellectual figure of the twentieth century."[7] His most influential works include *The Religion of Java* (1960); *Person, Time, and Conduct in Bali* (1966); *The Interpretation of Cultures* (1973); *Local Knowledge: Further Essays in Interpretive Anthropology* (1983); and

Works and Lives: The Anthropologist as Author (1988).[8]

Author's Background

Clifford Geertz wrote *The Interpretation of Cultures* in the 1960s, a period of upheaval in society and politics. In particular, these years were marked by postcolonialism* (a theoretical current relating to the various social, philosophical, and linguistic legacies of the colonial period) and social revolutions* (active, popular expressions of discontent with existing social systems). In the wake of these revolutions, "anthropology was torn apart by questions about its colonial past."[9]

To understand this past, we need to look back to the seventeenth and the eighteenth centuries. Anthropologists in the colonial era were dedicated to "scientifically" researching the cultures of the colonies. But they approached their inquiries with a bias that read Europeans and European society as biologically and culturally superior to all others, seeing colonized people as undeveloped and in need of being "civilized." This facilitated the rise in imperialism in Western Europe through the nineteenth and early twentieth centuries, as regimes used these theories to justify the expansion of their colonial empires.

In the early twentieth century, colonial administrations tasked anthropologists with studying the colonized, including addressing specific questions such as how the colonized people responded to colonial policies, such as the imposition of certain taxes.[10] Again, this was "science" in the service of a particular end, not objective inquiry.

Many colonial territories achieved independence after the Declaration on the Granting of Independence to Colonial Countries and Peoples, adopted by the United Nations in 1960. People began to question the involvement of anthropologists in colonialism and the relevance and ethics of the field in general.[11] This was the background against which Geertz conducted his anthropological work.

NOTES

1   Institute for Advanced Study, "Clifford Geertz 1926–2006," accessed December 8, 2015, https://www.ias.edu/news/press-releases/2009-49.

2   Aram Yengoyan, "Clifford Geertz, Cultural Portraits, and Southeast Asia," *The Journal of Asian Studies* 68, no. 4 (November 2009): 1215–17.

3   Andrew Yarrow, "Clifford Geertz, Cultural Anthropologist, Is Dead at 80," *New York Times*, November 1, 2006, accessed December 8, 2015, http://www.nytimes.com/2006/11/01/obituaries/01geertz.html?pagewanted=print&_r=0.

4   Institute for Advanced Study, "Geertz."

5   Clifford Geertz, "Passage and Accident: A Life of Learning," in *Available Light: Anthropological Reflections on Philosophical Topics*, by Clifford Geertz (Princeton: Princeton University Press, 2000), 7.

6   Clifford Geertz, *The Interpretation of Cultures*, 2nd edn (New York: Basic Books, 2000), 89.

7   Institute for Advanced Study, "Geertz."

8   See Clifford Geertz, *The Religion of Java* (Glencoe: The Free Press, *1960*); *Person, Time, and Conduct in Bali: An Essay in Cultural Analysis* (New Haven: Yale University Southeast Asia Studies, 1966); *Local Knowledge: Further Essays in Interpretive Anthropology* (New York: Basic Books, 1983); *Works and Lives: The Anthropologist as Author* (Stanford: Stanford University Press, 1988).

9   Institute for Advanced Study, "Geertz."

10 For a critical history of colonial anthropology, see Diane Lewis, "Anthropology and Colonialism," *Current Anthropology* 14, no. 5 (December 1973): 581–602.

11 Lewis, "Anthropology and Colonialism," 581.

MODULE 2
ACADEMIC CONTEXT

KEY POINTS

- Anthropology concerns itself with the study of human cultures.

- In 1871 the English anthropologist Sir Edward Burnett Tylor* laid the foundations of cultural anthropology* with his famous book *Primitive Culture*.[1]

- Like his academic predecessors, Geertz believed in the continued importance of anthropology as an academic discipline. Unlike prior academics, he believed that anthropologists must interpret other cultures not from the outside, but from the cultures' own point of view.

The Work in Its Context

When Clifford Geertz wrote *The Interpretation of Cultures* (1973), a new generation of scholars was emerging, holding the belief that anthropologists ought to study a culture from the perspectives of the people living in that culture. Colonial anthropologists had studied cultures "objectively from the outside." They believed that only European colonizers had the scientific capacity to discern a people's culture.[2] Geertz wrote his book at a time when anthropologists were beginning to challenge these colonial practices and perspectives.

To achieve "insider" understanding, anthropologists of the new generation lived in the midst of the subjects of their studies. Scholars call this participant observation.* These participant-anthropologists carefully recorded every small detail regarding the culture of the people and their communal lives, and attempted to explain their meanings. Scholars call this process and the reports that result

❝ [The essays that comprise *The Interpretation of Cultures*] all argue, sometimes explicitly, more often merely through the particular analysis they develop, for a narrowed, specialized, and, so I imagine, theoretically more powerful concept of culture to replace E. B. Tylor's famous 'most complex whole', which, its originative power not denied, seems to me to have reached the point where it obscures a good deal more than it reveals. ❞

Clifford Geertz, *The Interpretation of Cultures*

ethnography.* To this day, anthropologists continue to explore cultural phenomena using ethnography.

In *The Interpretation of Cultures*, Geertz put forward a particular approach to doing ethnography. He based it on his conceptualization of culture as a collection of symbols and symbolic rites that have specific meaning. Geertz's particular approach to understanding and researching culture helped anthropology distance itself from its colonial heritage and reinvent itself as a discipline.

The Interpretation of Cultures also helped to define a specific branch of anthropology—cultural anthropology. This usually refers to ethnographic works that are holistic* in spirit (aiming, that is, to provide a rounded, integrated view of a people's knowledge, customs, and practices). *The Interpretation of Cultures* contributed to an emerging trend of modern cultural anthropology in the twentieth-century United States. In the 1960s it became known as the symbolic or interpretive anthropology movement.

Overview of the Field

Until *The Interpretation of Cultures*, anthropologists had rooted their definition of culture in the British anthropologist Edward Burnett

Tylor's concept of the term. In 1871, Tylor defined culture as "that complex whole that includes knowledge, belief, art, morals, law, custom and any other capabilities and habits acquired by man as a member of a society."[3] This explanation is the backbone of anthropology's modern concept of culture.

In the 1920s and 1930s, the German-born American anthropologist Franz Boas* significantly shaped the discipline in the United States. Boas believed that anthropologists should conduct in-depth research on specific cultures. He was convinced that each society exists as a collective representation of its unique historical past. This theoretical approach was called "historical particularism."*

In the meantime, Bronisław Malinowski* of Poland and Alfred Radcliffe-Brown* of England had become major figures in modern European anthropology. Their way of researching culture involved analyzing how cultural conventions ensure that a society functions. For that reason, their theoretical approach was called functionalism.* A functionalist study, for instance, would examine initiation ceremonies for adolescents. According to functionalism, initiation ceremonies served as a rite of passage into adulthood, and so their unique characteristics took on that function within a particular society.

In the 1950s, an influential anthropologist from France, Claude Lévi-Strauss,* advocated a theoretical and methodological approach called structuralism.* Structuralism focused on the contrasting relationship between the elements of a system. For example, Lévi-Strauss suggested that most prevalent cultural patterns—such as those apparent in language, ritual, and myth— could be ordered in sets of opposing concepts, such as black and white, male and female, or day and night.

Geertz rejected Boas's theory of culture. He found it too broad—covering too many areas—and too universal, because it was rooted in Tylor's definition of culture as applying to all people, everywhere. Geertz referred to it as "a conceptual morass."[4] He also never completely accepted the European anthropologists' proposition that cultural practices serve particular functions. Geertz agreed with Lévi-Strauss on the importance of symbols and symbolic action, but he disagreed with his method for examining them. In contrast to Lévi-Strauss, Geertz believed that symbols—but not their contrasting relationships—could explain social context. Geertz argued that symbols derive their meanings not from their relationships with each other, but from the roles they play in people's lives.

Academic Influences

Geertz studied for his PhD at Harvard University in Cambridge, Massachusetts, which had just established an interdisciplinary* Department of Social Relations. His studies there shaped Geertz's intellectual development significantly. Its influence can clearly be seen in his essays in *The Interpretation of Cultures.* Geertz recognized early that insights gained in a variety of disciplines in the social sciences, arts, and humanities—such as language, philosophy, sociology,* history, and literature—could help explain and analyze phenomena in anthropology. So he drew on all these disciplines to examine the meanings embodied in symbols.[5]

At Harvard, Geertz studied with the anthropologist Clyde Kluckhohn,* who introduced him to cultural anthropology. Kluckhohn also contributed to Geertz's lifelong preoccupation with symbols and symbolic action and their role in embodying patterns of meaning. The sociologist Talcott Parsons* also played a significant role in Geertz's development at Harvard. Parsons introduced Geertz to the work of Max Weber,* a German sociologist. Gilbert Ryle,* an English philosopher of language, also influenced Geertz. Ryle concluded that the way the mind works is not different from the actions of the body. In other words, the mental vocabulary is simply another way to describe action. Scholars consider Weber one of the three founding architects of sociology, together with the French thinker Émile Durkheim* and the German political philosopher Karl Marx.* Weber's social theory informed Geertz's interpretive approach to meaning. Geertz particularly adopted the Weberian belief that scholars cannot interpret people's actions unless they understand the meanings individuals attach to those actions.

NOTES

1   See Edward Burnett Tylor, *Primitive Culture: Researches into the Development of Mythology, Philosophy, Religion, Language, Art and Custom,* 2 vols. (London: John Murray, 1871).

2   Institute for Advanced Study, "Clifford Geertz 1926–2006," accessed December 8, 2015, https://www.ias.edu/news/press-releases/2009-49.

3   Joan Leopold, *Culture in Comparative and Evolutionary Perspective: E. B. Tylor and the Making of Primitive Culture* (Berlin: Dietrich Reimer Verlag, 1980).

4   Clifford Geertz, *The Interpretation of Cultures*, 2nd edn. (New York: Basic Books, 2000), 4.

5   Clifford Geertz, "Passage and Accident: A Life of Learning," in *Available Light: Anthropological Reflections on Philosophical Topics*, by Clifford Geertz (Princeton: Princeton University Press, 2000), 7.

MODULE 3
THE PROBLEM

KEY POINTS

- Geertz's book redefines culture and the task of anthropologists.

- At the time when Geertz was writing, most anthropologists argued that culture was universal and could be found in social structures.

- Geertz significantly modified the theories of the mainstream debate, narrowing the dominant concept of culture.

Core Question

In *The Interpretation of Cultures* (1973), Clifford Geertz sought to address anthropology's need to redefine the concept of culture. In doing this, he hoped to reassert the usefulness of anthropology as an academic discipline. Geertz wrote *The Interpretation of Cultures* to offer a new conceptualization of culture as "a system of inherited conceptions expressed in symbolic forms by means of which men communicate, perpetuate, and develop their knowledge about and attitudes toward life."[1] In other words, Geertz wanted to define culture narrowly as the pattern of meaning that can be found in symbols and symbolic action.

Symbols such as a white dove or symbolic actions such as a smile signify ideas and represent qualities that have different, much deeper meaning than the literal meaning of the object or gesture. For example, as a symbol the white dove represents peace; a smile may symbolize the feeling of affection the smiler has for the person he or she smiles at. Symbols change their meanings based on the situation in which

> ❝ It is to this cutting of the culture concept down to size, therefore actually insuring its continued importance rather than undermining it, that the essays below are all, in their several ways and from their several directions, dedicated. ❞
>
> Clifford Geertz, *The Interpretation of Cultures*

they are being used. For instance, a chain can symbolize both "union" and "imprisonment." Therefore, the symbolic meaning of an action or an item hinges on the time, place, and manner in which it is used, and who "reads" it.

Geertz argued that particularly important symbols or rituals reflect a whole culture. For example, Geertz set out to demonstrate that the culture of the Balinese in Indonesia can be understood by comprehending the dynamics of their local ritual of putting on cockfights and betting on the fighting birds. He reports that the Balinese man sees the fighting bird as his "ideal self" and the fight as an arena that represents social tensions. Geertz believed that symbols get their meanings from the roles they play in people's lives, which is why we must study them as phenomena. He believed the main task of anthropologists should be unraveling and interpreting the meanings of symbols.

The Participants

Few anthropologists of Geertz's generation agreed about the definition of culture. Geertz's contemporary Roger Keesing,* an influential American cultural anthropologist, identifies four distinct approaches to the "rethinking of culture" in the 1960s.[2]

The first approach viewed culture as interrelated parts that form an overarching structure. The most notable proponent of that approach, the French scholar Claude Lévi-Strauss,* held that many common cultural patterns have their roots in basic structures of the mind. Lévi-Strauss believed that patterns of human thought produce the cultural categories that organize our world views. He argued, for instance, that the human mind has the impulse to categorize opposite concepts, such as light and dark or female and male. According to Lévi-Strauss, these essential conceptual patterns form the foundation for culture. This highly popular structuralist* approach dominated anthropological scholarship at the time.

Second, the American scholars Marshall Sahlins* and Roy Rappaport* proposed ecological approaches that viewed cultures as adaptive systems. An adaptive system, a set of interconnected parts that form a unified whole, responds and adapts to environmental changes. Examples of adaptive systems include natural ecosystems or human communities. Ecological anthropologists* study the relationship between humans and their biophysical environment. They examine how people adapt to their surroundings to survive and maintain themselves.

The third approach to the rethinking of culture at the time held that cultures were cognitive systems (that is, related to people's mental knowledge). Scholars such as Charles Frake* and James Spradley* attempted to formalize a view of culture as patterns of shared knowledge. Cognitive anthropology* examines what people from different groups know, and how that knowledge shapes the way they perceive and relate to the world around them.

The fourth approach to redefining the concept of culture viewed culture as an ensemble of symbolic systems. The pioneers of this approach included Louis Dumont* and Victor Turner* in Europe, and Clifford Geertz and David Schneider* in the United States. Symbolic anthropologists* examined rituals and symbols for their specific cultural meanings. Their studies usually explored the meanings of a particularly significant ritual or symbol, and attempted to show how it reflects an entire culture.

The Contemporary Debate

Geertz argued that cultural context influences the specific meaning of symbols. His concern with "the particular, the circumstantial, the concrete" echoed American anthropologist Franz Boas's* emphasis on particular cultures.[3] Decades earlier, Boas had proposed that anthropologists should research particular cultures and their histories. This contrasted with the then prevailing feeling that anthropologists should attempt to understand the evolution of all humankind.

Geertz acknowledged the relevance of social structures and their functions, as proposed by the European anthropologists Bronisław Malinowski* and Alfred Radcliffe-Brown.* But he distinguished between culture on the one hand and social structure on the other. To Geertz, social structure covers the political, economic, and social relations among people. Culture, on the other hand, signifies the context in which people live.

In *The Interpretation of Cultures*, Geertz most directly took on one of the then key figures in cultural anthropology, the structuralist thinker Claude Lévi-Strauss. Geertz accused Lévi-Strauss of so simplifying complex cultures that he minimized, obscured, and distorted them. Geertz argued that a structuralist approach looked only for schematic relationships. But in his view symbols derive their meanings not from their relationships with each other but from the roles they play in people's lives. Geertz also profoundly disagreed with the structuralist preoccupation with cultural universals that apply everywhere or in all cases. He believed Lévi-Strauss "annuls history, reduces sentiment to a shadow of the intellect, and replaces the particular minds of particular savages in particular jungles with the Savage Mind immanent [inherent] in us all."[4]

> 66 In anthropology, or anyway social anthropology, what the practitioners do is ethnography. And it is in understanding what ethnography is, or more exactly what doing ethnography is, that a start can be made toward grasping what anthropological analysis amounts to as a form of knowledge. 99
>
> Clifford Geertz, *The Interpretation of Cultures*

"expose their normalness without reducing their particularity."[5] Geertz proposed to do this by looking at symbols and symbolic acts—for him, these things represented a culture. He explored what symbolic actions like cockfighting signify for people within a culture—what their "shared meaning is." By doing this, he believed anthropologists can show what such knowledge "demonstrates about the society in which it is found and, beyond that, about social life as such."[6]

For instance, Geertz found that cockfights in the Indonesian province of Bali are not merely entertainment: they cannot be explained by reference to their literal purposes alone. Instead, cockfighting in Bali is a symbolic act: the cocks have metaphorical significance as symbolic representatives of their owners. Balinese men do not engage in cockfighting for the prize money: they do so because a win asserts their social status.

The Balinese remain obsessed with status because they see the cosmos as a grand hierarchy. Derived from Polynesian title ranks and Hindu castes (social classes), this hierarchy places animals and demons at the bottom of the pile and kings and gods at the top. Common humans sit in between those two extremes; a complicated array of ranks assigns a fixed status to everyone. This grand hierarchy forms the moral backbone of Balinese society. Cockfights display (and actualize) the way the Balinese perceive themselves and their social surroundings.

Approach

Geertz organized the book's 15 essays into five parts that set out the framework for his new way of studying culture. This allowed him to systematically build his argument for an interpretive anthropology.

In the first two parts of his work, Geertz draws on philosophy, literary theory, and sociology. He carefully establishes his theoretical base for defining culture as the meaning embodied in a collection of symbols or clusters of symbolic action. Geertz uses parts three and four of *The Interpretation of Cultures* to examine two specific cultural systems: religion and ideology.

Here, Geertz's focus "shifts from the question of how culture in general provides the human organism with the ordered forms without which it could not think or feel to the question of how specific cultures, in their specific symbolic formations, provide their members with specific systems of meaning and order within which to live their lives."[7] For example, Geertz argued that religion is a specific cultural system, comprising a specific set of symbols. These symbols outline a general order of existence, or the "really real." To Geertz, religious symbols act as vehicles for conceptualizing the "really real." To study them is to bring the particular religion into focus.

Geertz provides a detailed description of the set of symbols that embody a specific cultural system. He also chronicles the behaviors and moods these symbols inspire, and the context within which they have meaning. This level of detail represents what Geertz calls a thick description. This was Geertz's own method of doing ethnography. Thick description allowed him to make explicit the patterns of meaning embodied in a particular set of symbols.

In the fifth and last part of *The Interpretation of Cultures*, Geertz applied his method to interpreting Bali's cultural forms.

In applying thick description to a cultural system, Geertz challenged the then dominant positivist* research tradition. In anthropology, the positivist theory of knowledge views social facts as objects that exist independently of people, the meanings people assign to them, and the action an observer takes in relation to them. Positivist explanations create propositions relating to those objects. These can be verified or proven by means of observation or experiment.

Contribution in Context

Geertz imported the interpretive trend begun by German sociologist Max Weber* into the discipline of anthropology. Weber's concept of *Verstehen** made much of the importance of the meanings that individuals attach to their own actions. The German word *verstehen* means to "understand in a deep way." Researchers arrive at such an in-depth understanding of individuals by putting themselves into the other person's shoes. They do this by interviewing individuals and smaller groups and by experiencing these people's culture directly. This allows the anthropologists to better understand and interpret the meaning within a culture. Previous generations of anthropologists assumed that one set of laws and values could apply to all human experience.

Weber's notion of *Verstehen* critically informed Geertz's attempt to understand cultural meaning from the subjective perspectives of the people whose culture it is[8] (that is, from their point of view, according to their particular context). By adopting Weber's *Verstehen*, Geertz introduced interpretivism* into contemporary anthropology. Interpretivism assumes that we cannot understand people's responses to a situation without knowing how the people themselves see that situation. Geertz's original theory gave *The Interpretation of Cultures* the reputation as "a major voice" of the interpretive anthropology movement of the 1960s.[9]

NOTES

1   Clifford Geertz, *The Interpretation of Cultures*, 2nd edn (New York: Basic Books 2000), v.

2   Geertz, *The Interpretation of Cultures*, vii.

3   Geertz, *The Interpretation of Cultures*, viii, ix.

4   Geertz, *The Interpretation of Cultures*, ix.

5   Geertz, *The Interpretation of Cultures*, 14.

6   Geertz, *The Interpretation of Cultures*, 26–7.

7   Sherry Ortner, "Clifford Geertz (1926–2006)," *American Anthropologist* 109, no. 4 (2007): 787.

8   Ortner, "Clifford Geertz (1926–2006)," 787.

9   Richard Shweder, "The Resolute Irresolution of Clifford Geertz," *Common Knowledge* 13, nos. 2–3 (Spring–Fall 2007): 191–205.

SECTION 2
IDEAS

MODULE 5
MAIN IDEAS

KEY POINTS

- Key themes in *The Interpretation of Cultures* include the nature of culture, the way it operates, and how scholars ought to study it.

- The text chiefly argues that culture resides in symbolic acts. These represent abstract ideas that must be interpreted within their particular social contexts.

- In his main argument Geertz unpicks the principal elements of culture.

Key Themes

In *The Interpretation of Cultures* (1973), Clifford Geertz argues for an understanding of culture as a system of shared meaning: the collective understanding held by members of the same society. As Geertz saw it, every society has symbols and symbolic actions that represent the main tenets of its shared meaning. Every state has a national flag, for example, that symbolizes the country. Such symbols and symbolic actions serve as signifiers, or vehicles, for the shared meaning that characterizes a particular culture. Geertz concluded that anthropologists gain insight into a culture by decoding particularly important symbols and symbolic action, such as myth and ritual. This decoding reveals the meaning that the symbols represent.

Geertz argued that in deciphering the meanings of symbols and symbolic actions anthropologists should read meanings as native people do within their particular social context. Anthropologists then need to translate and interpret these meanings to outsiders. Geertz explained that anthropologists can only achieve this by immersing

> ❝ The concept of culture I espouse, and whose utility the essays below attempt to demonstrate, is essentially a semiotic one. Believing, with Max Weber, that man is an animal suspended in webs of significance he himself has spun, I take culture to be those webs, and the analysis of it to be therefore not an experimental science in search of law but an interpretive one in search of meaning. ❞
>
> Clifford Geertz, *The Interpretation of Cultures*

themselves in the culture they study. Immersion allows anthropologists to describe in detail the everyday life and practices they observe, and to determine their social ground and import. Geertz termed this particular process of ethnography* thick description.* He took this term from the work of the British philosopher Gilbert Ryle.*

Geertz conceived of thick description as a way of explaining the cultural context of actions, words, and objects and the meaning people place on them. Thick description offers enough context that a person outside the culture can make sense of the behavior. Thin description, by contrast, states facts without such meaning or significance. In *The Interpretation of Cultures*, Geertz proposed anthropologists should consider their principal tasks to be providing thick description and interpreting it to outsiders.[1]

Exploring the Ideas

Claiming that "man is an animal suspended in webs of significance he himself has spun, [and] I take culture to be those webs," Geertz explained that people shape the patterns of their behaviors and give meaning and significance to their way of life.[2] These meanings, or webs of significance, are the collective property of a group of people— and what we call "culture."

People rely on these shared meanings to sustain their social life.

They embody these shared meanings in public symbols and symbolic action so insiders can learn and share them—and outsiders can recognize them. Symbols and symbolic action also transmit meaning, communicating coded messages that help people identify how they should view themselves and others, and how they should feel about the world.

By focusing on the central role of symbols and symbolic action in capturing, carrying, and transmitting the web of shared meaning we call culture, Geertz put forward a semiotic* concept of culture—one rooted in signs and symbols that epitomize the abstract ideas they stand for. Geertz's semiotic concept of culture saw that the meaning of a symbol is not set in stone. It can vary based on the context and the motivation of the person who acts.

Given this, Geertz argued that the anthropologist must spell out "the implicit or unstated presuppositions, implications, or meaning that make this or that action, practice, object, or pattern of sounds intelligible to members of some culture or interpretive community in some specific context."[3] In other words, the anthropologist unravels the web of meaning that a symbol or symbolic action presents within a particular context, and then translates and conveys it to outsiders.

According to Geertz, this task is much like trying to read an ensemble of texts with the anthropologist straining "to read over the shoulders of those to whom [these texts] properly belong."[4] To him, interpreting "culture as text" constituted the very essence of thick description. The English philosopher of language Gilbert Ryle identified a difference between a "thick description" that takes account of the circumstances, and a "thin description" that has no context.[5]

Ryle gives the example of someone "rapidly raising and lowering their right eyelid"—the physical act of winking. The person could suffer from an uncontrollable twitch; he or she could have done it on purpose in order to interact with someone else, for example to catch their attention; or the person could have winked in order to make fun of someone with a nervous twitch. It all hinges on the circumstances and the intentions of the individual who is winking. This implies that communication, description, and explanation cannot clearly be separated. All except the most trivial descriptions of human actions and behavior involve interpretations, expectations, and explanations of why people acted the way they did and what they were seeking to achieve in doing so. Geertz argues, in essence, that we must pay attention to the *full* meaning of people's actions before we can believe we understand them.

Language and Expression

Geertz set out his treatise systematically by arguing "sometimes explicitly, more often merely through the particular analysis … for a narrowed, specialized, and … theoretically more powerful concept of culture."[6] To that end, the essays in *The Interpretation of Cultures* first defined culture, then examined two specific cultural systems, and finally applied Geertz's method of thick description to interpreting a particular ritual.

Despite the author's effort to be systematic, critics have found *The Interpretation of Cultures* complex and somewhat difficult to follow. Geertz's entertaining and poetic writing style does not help. It tends to be stylistically peculiar, putting its point across in metaphors and anecdotes as opposed to simple explanations. In fact, one critic, referencing a nineteenth-century English novelist, described Geertz as the "Jane Austen* of ethnography."[7] The American philosopher Richard Rorty* described Geertz's writing as "self-conscious exhibitions and commentaries on the very process of thought."[8]

As a result, general-interest readers have frequently misunderstood and misinterpreted *The Interpretation of Cultures*. Geertz's student Sherry Ortner* noted that one obituary described Geertz's ideas as "covered in fuzz" and bemoaned that he turned anthropology "into a lame and confused form of literary scholarship."[9]

NOTES

1   Richard Shweder, "Clifford Geertz," *Proceedings of the American Philosophical Society* 154, no. 1 (March 2010): 90.

2   Clifford Geertz, *The Interpretation of Cultures*, 2nd edn (New York: Basic Books, 2000), 5.

3   Geertz, *The Interpretation of Cultures*, 10.

4   Geertz, *The Interpretation of Cultures*, 452.

5   Gilbert Ryle, *The Concept of Mind* (Chicago: University of Chicago Press, 1949).

6   Geertz, *The Interpretation of Cultures*, viii.

7   Renato Rosaldo Jr., "Geertz's Gifts," *Common Knowledge* 13, nos. 2–3 (2007): 208.

8   Richard Shweder and Byron Good, eds., *Clifford Geertz by His Colleagues* (Chicago: University of Chicago Press, 2005), 50.

9   Sherry Ortner, "Clifford Geertz (1926–2006)," *American Anthropologist* 109, no. 4 (2007): 788.

MODULE 6
SECONDARY IDEAS

KEY POINTS

- Geertz's two main secondary ideas involve his interpretations of religion and ideology as cultural systems.

- Geertz was far ahead of his time with his theories on religion and ideology as specific systems of meaning.

- With today's societies becoming more divided along religious and ideological lines, Geertz's theories still have much to contribute to current debates.

Other Ideas

Clifford Geertz's *The Interpretation of Cultures* contains two significant secondary ideas—religion and ideology as two specific "meaning systems." Geertz used these to illustrate his core thesis.

Geertz shows how both religion and ideology provide people with particular systems of meaning and help them order their lives.[1] Religion, he proposes, is a cultural system devoted to defining what is "really real" for people;[2] it is a set of symbols that creates compelling and enduring feelings in people by setting out a general order of existence: the way things are, on both the cosmic and material level. These conceptions were clothed with factuality—that is, they were presented as facts; in this way, the feelings created by the system of symbols were made to appear uniquely real and tangible.[3]

Geertz examined ideology the same way. He claimed that, just like religion, it serves as "an ordered system of cultural symbols" that establishes directions to help people find their way.[4] People use ideology's symbolic systems to express political faith in a set of ideas;

> ❝ To look at the symbolic dimensions of social action—art, religion, ideology, science, law, morality, common sense—is not to turn away from the existential dilemmas of life for some empyrean* realm of de-emotionalized forms; it is to plunge into the midst of them. ❞
>
> Clifford Geertz, *The Interpretation of Cultures*

these ideas might concern social arrangements, institutional power, organizational frameworks, and governing elites. Geertz notes that people embrace an ideological "meaning system" to ease their tensions. These tensions may stem from, among other things, watching the world or losing social and political orientation. Ideologies appeal to our emotional desire to believe in larger-than-life possibilities. They serve as both an expression of our hope and a reflection of our despair.

Geertz illuminated his argument by interpreting ideological developments in the 66 countries that achieved political independence from colonial rule between 1945 and 1968. He demonstrated how ideological parties manipulated the meaning of symbols according to the needs of a particular society and the demands of its historical situation.

Exploring the Ideas

Geertz argued that, in a world in which man's life has "no genuine order at all—no empirical regularity, no emotional form, no moral coherence," religion serves as a central cultural system to reassure people. Through its symbols, religion presents "an image of … a genuine order of the world, which will account for, and even celebrate, the perceived ambiguities, puzzles, and paradoxes."[5] In other words, Geertz suggests religion exists to comfort people and assure them that everything has an order.

To achieve this, "sacred symbols function to synthesize a people's ethos ... and their world view."[6] At its heart, then, a religious perspective enables people to feel a connection between how life should be (as specified by the religion in question) and the way things really are.

Geertz illustrated this point by discussing the funeral of a young boy in Java who had died suddenly. The ritual failed to achieve its purpose of producing *iklas*,* acceptance of death, and *rukun*,* communal harmony. Instead, it stoked communal tension. Geertz considered that the funeral rites failed for several reasons.

The first reason for this failure was that, because of conflict between a local official and the political party with which the boy's family was affiliated, the community did not follow the usual Islamic procedures. The second reason involved improvised modifications created to allow the funeral to proceed; instead of coming to a collective consensus about ways to alter the funeral rite, one individual took charge and made the changes unilaterally. The conflict that arose at the funeral, in Geertz's view, stemmed from a burgeoning gap between the community's cultural beliefs and social interaction in real life.

Geertz saw the role of ideology as "justificatory" and "apologetic": it establishes and defends patterns of belief and value.[7] To Geertz, ideologies seek only selective questions and answers, and target only narrow problems. That leads them to underestimate or exaggerate social realities. For example, the widespread ideology of anti-Semitism*—hostility toward Jewish people—in Europe of the 1930s and 1940s placed the blame for social and economic problems on one target enemy: Jews. Geertz advocated an analytical framework to examine ideologies as something other than weapons that different interests use in an ongoing struggle for power. He observed that the term "ideology" had taken on an "evaluative" connotation, which made it into a diagnosis of social, political, and intellectual diseases that diverted societies from a sensible appreciation of reality.

In the aftermath of the World War II,* and in the midst of the long period of global tension known as the Cold War* and the political turmoil that followed the end of the colonial period in many nations, particularly in Africa, Asia, and the Caribbean, Geertz sensed that ideology actually "draws its persuasive power from any discrepancy between what is believed and what can, now or someday, be established as scientifically correct."⁸ Accordingly, he noted that the social sciences needed to develop a "genuinely non-evaluative conception of ideology" (a conception that does not seek to establish the soundness of any ideology), capable of taking social and psychological contexts into account.⁹ This proposition offered a route to defining "ideology" in a way that social scientists in general could find useful.

Overlooked

Despite the dense and complex argument Geertz puts forward in *The Interpretation of Cultures,* we may argue that all significant aspects have been examined and discussed. Many scholars have offered their differing perspectives on one aspect or another of the book in the past 40 years. Indeed, as one reviewer puts it, "to criticize Geertz has become an anthropological obsession, almost a rite of passage."¹⁰

Scholars have focused their attention on many things. These include the volume's view of culture as intrinsic to evolution, its theory on particular "meaning systems," its method of thick description,* its regional focus and ethnographies,* its neglect of important modern concepts and theories, its implications for disciplines beyond anthropology, its deliberation of issues of social and moral philosophy, and even its literary flair.¹¹

Reconsidering the text against the background of contemporary political events, social problems, and historical developments may yield new and interesting insights. But it will not significantly change the way in which we understand *The Interpretation of Cultures* as a whole. For this same reason, Geertz chose not to change anything of substance to improve or update his arguments before publication in

1973—more than a decade after he wrote the essays. And certainly much had happened in the world and in anthropology by the time he republished the work in 2000. Yet still he made no substantive changes. As Geertz put it, "some of the hares I started then have turned out to be worth chasing."[12]

NOTES

1   Sherry Ortner, "Clifford Geertz (1926–2006)," *American Anthropologist* 109, no. 4 (2007): 787.

2   Clifford Geertz, *The Interpretation of Cultures*, 2nd edn (New York: Basic Books, 2000), 112.

3   Geertz, *The Interpretation of Cultures*, 90.

4   Geertz, *The Interpretation of Cultures*, 196.

5   Geertz, *The Interpretation of Cultures*, 107–8.

6   Geertz, *The Interpretation of Cultures*, 89.

7   Geertz, *The Interpretation of Cultures*, 231.

8   Geertz, *The Interpretation of Cultures*, 72.

9   Geertz, *The Interpretation of Cultures*, 196.

10 E. Bruner, "Book Review: Clifford Geertz: His Critics and Followers, 1998," *Anthropology and Humanism* 23, no. 2 (1998): 216.

11 Ortner, "Clifford Geertz (1926–2006)," 787.

12 Geertz, *The Interpretation of Cultures*, vi.

MODULE 7
ACHIEVEMENT

KEY POINTS

- Geertz successfully set out a "treatise in cultural theory."

- The publication of *The Interpretation of Cultures* coincided neatly with anthropology's need to reinvent itself as a discipline.

- *The Interpretation of Cultures* remains relevant across place, time, and cultures, both in and beyond the discipline of anthropology.

Assessing the Argument

In the early 1970s, Clifford Geertz's publisher asked him to select a set of his essays and arrange them into the book that would become *The Interpretation of Cultures*. At first, he remained unsure about what his intention should be. Most of the essays resulting from several years of fieldwork in Indonesia fell into the category Geertz called "empirical studies" (that is, studies based on information verifiable by observation). He eventually decided to include all his essays that "bear, directly and explicitly, on the concept of culture" and how to study such a concept.[1] He wanted to share with the world his definition of culture as webs of meaning as well as his interpretive* approach to studying these webs.

To do this, he had to explain and translate the subjective and contextual meanings of the people whose culture it is. Geertz felt that "it is in understanding what ethnography* is, or more exactly what doing ethnography is, that a start can be made toward grasping what anthropological analysis amounts to as a form of knowledge"[2] ("ethnography" refers to research exploring cultural phenomena,

> **"** Certain ideas burst upon the intellectual landscape with a tremendous force. They resolve so many fundamental problems at once that they seem also to promise that they will resolve all fundamental problems, clarify all obscure issues. **"**
>
> Clifford Geertz, *The Interpretation of Cultures*

documented in written field studies or case studies). In showcasing the scientific knowledge his interpretive study of culture produced, Geertz also wanted to highlight the relevance of anthropology as a discipline.

It is fair to say that the argument Geertz put forward in *The Interpretation of Cultures* achieved its goal. The volume's call to understand the human condition "as defined by the constant production and transformation of meaning" proved critical to the evolution of the intellectual environment.[3] It caused a fundamental shift in the discipline's aims and methods often referred to as the "interpretive turn" in anthropology.[4] Geertz's "treatise in cultural theory" not only offered a new definition of culture (the central, unifying concept of anthropology as it was practiced in the United States) but also successfully established that we ought to study culture by interpreting the subjective meanings that people in any given culture ascribe to their social action.

Geertz's collection of essays also succeeded in challenging the then dominant idea of culture as universal and all-encompassing. It called into question the value of positivist* approaches to studying culture, which maintained that social facts exist independent of people and their meanings. It also presented an alternative to structuralist* and functionalist* approaches, both of which looked only at meaning embedded in structures; functionalist approaches consider all aspects of social and cultural behavior to be "organs," so to speak, serving some vital function in the "organism" of a society. Geertz's method of thick description* came to define not only his method of ethnography but also those of cultural anthropologists in general.

Achievement in Context

The Interpretation of Cultures hit bookstores as anthropology struggled to reinvent itself as a discipline. Practitioners had begun to question and rethink the core concept of culture put forward by previous generations. Geertz's ideas shaped the new definition of American cultural anthropology.

The Interpretation of Cultures did much to cement cultural anthropology as a respected and valued subdivision of anthropology in its own right. It separated the discipline from biological anthropology* (the study of human evolution), linguistic anthropology* (the study of language and how it represents culture), and archaeological anthropology* (the study of the historical traces of human culture) in the United States, and from social anthropology* (the study of social structures and their role in human cultures) in the United Kingdom. It gave cultural anthropology a rationale for the era following the end of the colonial period* and inspired the growth of modern cultural comparative studies—studies that seek to understand cultures by examining their differences and similarities.

The book had its most direct impact on the wider intellectual environment as a proponent of an interpretive movement in anthropology. Many scholars remained unconvinced by Geertz's exclusive emphasis on symbols. But they considered *The Interpretation of Cultures* to be the reference for interpretive inquiry. A seminal book, it influenced ideas about theory and method across many academic disciplines. The most influential social science books frequently cited it. Translated into 20 languages, the work has turned Geertz into "a true giant of social and cultural theory."[5]

Limitations

Today we grapple with social problems such as cyberbullying* and global warming* that Geertz could not have foreseen when he wrote *The Interpretation of Cultures* 40 years ago. This "limitation" is, perhaps, inevitable. For his "treatise in culture" Geertz typically studied static, small-scale, homogeneous (internally similar), and relatively isolated societies.[6] By contrast, modern cultures are fluid and characterized by a lack of unity. The identities and subjectivities*—interpretations of experience that differ according to our various identities—dissolve in the many webs of meaning that make up every present-day culture; men, women, Muslims, Buddhists, drug addicts, teetotalers, homosexuals, heterosexuals, bisexuals (to name just a few) contribute differently to the formation of these many webs of meaning.

Today people consider themselves part of multiple cultures. They may share a culture with their particular ethnic group, the country they live in, the organization they work for, their social class, their religious community, or their virtual friends*—the list can go on and on. In today's world culture is neither bounded nor isolated. Any one person can be just as much part of any particular culture as he or she would like. People have internalized an assemblage of different meaning fragments from a range of cultures, or meaning systems, at any point in time.[7] This makes "culture" even more difficult to define than it was when Geertz wrote this work.

NOTES

1 Clifford Geertz, *The Interpretation of Cultures*, 2nd edn (New York: Basic Books, 2000), vii.

2 Geertz, *The Interpretation of Cultures*, 5–6.

3 Sherry Ortner, "Clifford Geertz (1926–2006)," *American Anthropologist* 109, no. 4 (2007): 787.

4   Sherry Ortner, "Special Issue: The Fate of 'Culture': Geertz and beyond,"
     Representations 59 (1997): 6.

5   Jeffrey Alexander et al., eds., *Interpreting Clifford Geertz: Cultural
     Investigation in the Social Sciences* (New York: Palgrave Macmillan, 2011),
     xiii.

6   Geertz, *The Interpretation of Cultures*, viii.

7   David Kronenfeld et al., eds., *A Companion to Cognitive Anthropology*
     (Singapore: Blackwell Publishing Ltd., 2011).

MODULE 8
PLACE IN THE AUTHOR'S WORK

KEY POINTS

- The chief focus of Geertz's life's work has been the rendition,* or translation, of culture.

- Considered a masterwork, *The Interpretation of Cultures* became Geertz's best-known publication.

- *The Interpretation of Cultures* established Geertz as one of the founding fathers of the interpretive* or symbolic movement.

Positioning

Before Clifford Geertz collected his essays and published them as *The Interpretation of Cultures*, he spent 10 years as professor of anthropology at the University of Chicago. In this period, from 1960 to 1970, Geertz focused his research on two Indonesian* islands, Java and Bali, resulting in three books: *Religion of Java* (1960), *Agricultural Involution* (1963), and *Peddlers and Princes* (also 1963).[1] During the sixties, Geertz conducted research in Morocco, and his work produced a number of publications, including a book in which he compares Indonesia and Morocco, entitled *Islam Observed* (1968).[2]

Geertz published *The Interpretation of Cultures* after taking a position as professor of social science at the Institute for Advanced Study at Princeton University. The book contained a selection of essays that Geertz had individually published throughout the sixties. Geertz purposely chose not to create a publication that would be a "review or autobiography of his career."[3] Instead, he looked to find a through-line in his work. As he combed through his essays, he decided that "the rendition [interpretation] of culture" had been his "most persistent

> ❝ Whether [Geertz] is revered or reviled, all those involved in cultural research have to be familiar with his work, just as all psychoanalytic thinkers must deal with Freud,* all critical theorists with Marx, and all structuralists* with Saussure.* ❞
>
> Jeffrey Alexander et al., *Interpreting Clifford Geertz: Cultural Investigation in the Social Sciences*

interest as an anthropologist."[4]

Although Geertz had changed his intellectual standpoint slightly over the years, he resisted the temptation to write his "changed view back into earlier works"[5] and left the essays' central arguments untouched. When the book, originally published in 1973, was reissued in 2000, the only substantive thing Geertz added to the original edition was an introductory chapter. This introduction outlined his general position and provided an overarching framework for the collection.[6]

Integration

The Interpretation of Cultures became Geertz's best-known publication, establishing him as one of the founding fathers of the interpretive or symbolic movement. In 1974 he further cemented this reputation by editing the anthology *Myth, Symbol, and Culture*.[7] That collection contained papers on symbolic anthropology* by a number of important anthropologists. During this period, Geertz also published ethnographic* studies, such as *Kinship in Bali* (1975) and—together with Hildred Geertz and Lawrence Rosen—*Meaning and Order in Moroccan Society* (1979).[8]

From the 1980s onward, Geertz published theoretical essays and reviews for the *New York Review of Books*. The books that he wrote during this period featured collected essays, including *Local Knowledge* (1983), *Available Light* (2000), and *Life Among The Anthros* (published posthumously in 2010).[9] He also published a volume with short essays on the method of ethnography, which was entitled *Works and Lives* (1988), as well as the autobiography *After the Fact* (1995).[10]

While we may certainly consider Geertz's body of work coherent, his views evolved during his long career. Critics argue that his intellectual journey charts three broad trends.[11] First, Geertz became increasingly convinced that no knowledge is universal. Instead, he determined that insights only hold true for a particular group of individuals. Second, Geertz became less worried about functionalism* (roughly, interpreting a culture by considering the useful "functions" that its various parts serve) and increasingly concerned with the need to study culture in semiotic* terms (that is, by interpreting symbols and language). Third, Geertz always grounded his approach in discrete, specific "cultural portraits." But it began to seem imperative to him "to think [more] in terms of 'cultures' (lowercase and multiple) than 'Culture' (capitalized and singular)."[12]

Significance

Geertz's body of work has influenced scholars from a range of disciplines. He had a profound impact on theory and method in anthropology, and in the fields of history, sociology,* religious studies, and cultural studies. Some joke that Geertz became so famous that he generated his own "cultural system."[13] The "Geertz culture" ties together key terms, such as thick description,* and frequently repeated quotes, images, and parables from his body of work. Critics argue that such reference capable of generating instantaneous recognition is found only very rarely and with the most influential thinkers, such as the pioneering sociologist Max Weber* and the notably influential political philosopher Karl Marx.*[14]

Lists of the most influential science books routinely cite Geertz's masterwork *The Interpretation of Cultures* alongside the French sociologist and anthropologist Pierre Bourdieu's* book *Distinction* and the American sociologist C. Wright Mills's* *The Sociological Imagination*.[15] In addition, *The Interpretation of Cultures* boasts an Amazon.com sales ranking of 8000, even though it first appeared more than 40 years ago, back when "Amazon" was merely a river.[16]

Interpretive or symbolic anthropology has proven to be a popular and influential school of thought within and beyond the discipline of anthropology. It remains as central to modern debates about globalization (the trend toward increasingly close cultural, economic, and political ties across continental boundaries) and cultural pluralism (the coexistence of several cultures in the same society) as it was 40 years ago to the debates on cultural appropriation (the acquisition of cultural habits, usually by a "dominant" culture).[17]

NOTES

1   Clifford Geertz, *The Religion of Java* (Glencoe: The Free Press, *1960*); *Agricultural Involution: The Processes of Ecological Change in Indonesia* (Los Angeles: University of California Press, 1963); *Peddlers and Princes: Social Development and Economic Change in Two Indonesian Towns* (Chicago: University of Chicago Press, 1963).

2   Clifford Geertz, *Islam Observed: Religious Development in Morocco and Indonesia* (New Haven: Yale University Press, 1968).

3   Clifford Geertz, *The Interpretation of Cultures,* 2nd edn (New York: Basic Books, 2000), viii.

4   Geertz, *The Interpretation of Cultures*, v.

5   Geertz, *The Interpretation of Cultures*, viii.

6   Geertz, *The Interpretation of Cultures*, ix.

7   Clifford Geertz, ed., *Myth, Symbol, and Culture* (New York: Norton, 1974).

8   Clifford Geertz, *Kinship in Bali* (Chicago: University of Chicago Press, 1975) and Clifford Geertz, Hildred Geertz, and Lawrence Rosen, *Meaning and Order in Moroccan Society* (New York: Cambridge University Press, 1979).

9   Clifford Geertz, *Local Knowledge: Further Essays in Interpretive Anthropology* (New York: Basic Books, 1983); *Available Light: Anthropological Reflections on Philosophical Topics* (Princeton: Princeton University Press, 2000); *Life*

among the Anthros and Other Essays (Princeton: Princeton University Press, 2010).

10 Clifford Geertz, *Works and Lives: The Anthropologist as Author* (Stanford: Stanford University Press, 1988); *After the Fact: Two Countries, Four Decades, One Anthropologist* (Cambridge, MA: Harvard University Press, 1995).

11 Aram Yengoyan, "Clifford Geertz, Cultural Portraits, and Southeast Asia," *The Journal of Asian Studies* 68, no. 4 (November 2009): 1215–16.

12 Yengoyan, "Clifford Geertz," 1216.

13 Jeffrey Alexander et al., eds., *Interpreting Clifford Geertz: Cultural Investigation in the Social Sciences* (New York: Palgrave Macmillan, 2011), xiii–xiv.

14 Alexander et al., eds., *Interpreting Clifford Geertz,* xiii–xiv.

15 Alexander et al., eds., *Interpreting Clifford Geertz,* xiii–xiv. See Pierre Bourdieu, *Distinction: A Social Critique of the Judgement of Taste,* translated by Richard Nice (Cambridge, MA: Harvard University Press, 1987) and C. Wright Mills, *The Sociological Imagination* (New York: Oxford University Press, 1959).

16 Alexander et al., eds., *Interpreting Clifford Geertz,* xiv.

17 Sherry Ortner, "Special Issue: The Fate of 'Culture': Geertz and beyond," *Representations* 59 (1997): 1–14.

SECTION 3
IMPACT

MODULE 9
THE FIRST RESPONSES

KEY POINTS

- The main criticism of Geertz's *The Interpretation of Cultures* revolved around the author's subjective interpretive* approach (his method of interpreting cultural features, as understood by the people that made up his cultural study, for outsiders), his focus on symbols, and his neglect of power, conflict, inequality, and historical processes.

- Addressing his critics, Geertz could only emphasize his different view on the nature of social life and the prospects of creating rules to explain human behavior.

- Scholars consider Geertz's work a productive place to start learning about an interpretive approach to culture.

Criticism

When Geertz published *The Interpretation of Cultures*, positivism* dominated the research tradition in anthropology. The positivist theory of knowledge holds that social facts exist independently of people and the contextual meanings people give to these facts. We can verify or prove these facts by means of observation or experiment. Positivist scholars argued that Geertz took an unscientific approach to culture. They felt he relied too much on interpretation, which led to "uncontrolled subjectivism"[1]—that is, his findings had more to do with his own understanding than with objective, verifiable "truth."

Even anthropologists who understood the benefits of an interpretive approach criticized *The Interpretation of Cultures*. They felt Geertz had invested in too narrow a semiotic* concept of culture—a concept that relies on the reading of meanings in signs and symbols.

❝ Indeed, to criticize Geertz has become an anthropological obsession, almost a rite of passage. **❞**

Edward Bruner, "Book Review: Clifford Geertz: His Critics and Followers, 1998"

For instance, some of Geertz's influential contemporaries opposed his symbolic approaches. Anthropologists such as Marvin Harris,* Roy Rappaport,* Marshall Sahlins,* and Andrew P. Vayda* argued instead that we should understand culture as a non-biological means humans use to adapt to life in different environments. Maintaining that all cultural phenomena arise in response to the practical problems of life on earth, these anthropologists criticized Geertz for neglecting power, conflict, and inequality. They also objected to his political and ethical neutrality.[2] For instance, when the anthropologist Talal Asad* examined Geertz's definition of religion, he found "it omits the crucial dimension of power" and "ignores the varying social conditions for the production of knowledge."[3]

Scholars of all convictions took issue with the explanatory reach of Geertz's seminal work. They pointed out "the explanation was based solely on the depth and detail of the description." In other words, Geertz had let culture describe and explain itself.[4] For instance, historians argued that Geertz's explanation of a system of meaning typically failed to consider "the historical processes that led to its production."[5] Talal Asad echoed this claim. He ended his critical evaluation of Geertz's account of religion with the plea to investigate religion "with reference to the historical conditions necessary for the existence of particular practices and discourses."[6]

Responses

Geertz never joined the scientific debates among anthropologists and did not make much effort to defend his work against critics. He justified his silence by reasoning that his main interest was to articulate "a positive program for anthropology."[7]

When pressed, he could only emphasize his different view on "the character of social life and the prospects of developing law-like explanatory statements about human behavior."[8] Geertz did not see human culture as a power "to which social events, behaviors, institutions, or processes can be causally attributed" by identifying schematic relationships and cultural universals.[9] Instead, Geertz understood culture as a context within which particular individuals construct systems of meaning. He stressed that "the whole point of a semiotic approach to culture is to aid us in gaining access to the conceptual world in which our subjects live so that we can, in some extended sense of the term, converse with them."[10]

Geertz also explained that most of the meanings that determine human behavior remain narrow in scope, limited to a particular local context. So he reasoned that social science generalizations will inevitably also be restricted in scope.[11] In his later work, Geertz further deepened his commitment to studying culture in a particularistic* and relativistic* way—that is, by considering every culture as a "particular" (singular) case in which beliefs, practices, and so on have no greater or lesser claim to validity or worth than those of any other culture (notably that of the anthropologist).

Conflict and Consensus

Many anthropologists remained unconvinced by Clifford Geertz's exclusive emphasis on symbols. But they considered it a sound starting point for an interpretive approach to culture, which needs to be supplemented by also considering other aspects that define a culture, such as history, power dynamics, and social structures, among other things.[12]

Significant consensus had formed around the importance of interpreting meaning from the acting person's subjective point of view. Questioning the then common positivist model, many agreed with Geertz's argument that it remains important to understand meaning based on context and the intention of the person who acts in specific situations. For that reason, scholars still see *The Interpretation of Cultures* as a powerful resource for those who want to go beyond positivist* data collection or grand structural* theories (theories that assume that a culture can be analyzed by identifying the relationship between the elements that compose its structure). Scholars find value in the book's proposition that anthropologists must study how people make sense of the world around them.

Despite its critics, *The Interpretation of Cultures* defined the central ideas of the discipline of American cultural anthropology.* That seems a powerful indicator of the consensus that the book generated. Geertz's work distinguished cultural anthropology from closely related approaches such as social anthropology,* which studies relationships between humans. It gave anthropology a new justification in the postcolonial* era. It also inspired the growth of the modern discipline of cultural comparative studies.

NOTES

1   Sherry Ortner, "Special Issue: The Fate of 'Culture': Geertz and beyond," *Representations* 59 (1997), 1–14.

2   Edward Bruner, "Book Review: Clifford Geertz: His Critics and Followers, 1998," *Anthropology and Humanism* 23, no. 2 (1998): 216.

3   Talal Asad, "Anthropological Conceptions of Religion: Reflections on Geertz," *Man* 18, no. 2 (1983): 237–59.

4   Aram Yengoyan, "Clifford Geertz, Cultural Portraits, and Southeast Asia," *The Journal of Asian Studies* 68, no. 4 (November 2009): 1217.

5   Bruner, "Book Review: Clifford Geertz: His Critics and Followers, 1998," 216.

6   Asad, "Anthropological Conceptions of Religion," 237.

7 Sherry Ortner, "Clifford Geertz (1926–2006)," *American Anthropologist* 109, no. 4 (2007): 788.

8 Richard Shweder, "The Resolute Irresolution of Clifford Geertz," *Common Knowledge* 13, nos. 2–3 (Spring 2007), 197.

9 Clifford Geertz, *The Interpretation of Cultures*, 2nd edn (New York: Basic Books, 2000), 14.

10 Geertz *The Interpretation of Cultures*, 24.

11 Shweder, "The Resolute Irresolution of Clifford Geertz," 196.

12 Bruner, "Book Review: Clifford Geertz: His Critics and Followers, 1998," 216.

MODULE 10
THE EVOLVING DEBATE

KEY POINTS

- Geertz's relativist* approach—his theoretical stand that no culture's beliefs and practices could lay claim to any particular validity—and his interpretation of alternative moral universes (other systems of morality) appealed to many scholars.

- Many credit *The Interpretation of Cultures* with popularizing an interpretive* school of thought.

- While cultural anthropologists* share an affinity for Geertz's interpretivism, they do not view cultures as bounded and isolated. So they supplement Geertz's approach by looking at wider political, economic, social, historical, and cultural frameworks that affect the ways in which local people assign meanings within their culture.

Uses and Problems

While many scholars remained unconvinced by Clifford Geertz's exclusive emphasis on symbols as codes for cultural meaning, the ideas he put forward in *The Interpretation of Cultures* proved very popular. In fact, scholars credit them with popularizing an interpretive school of thought. They have also affected the direction of thinking in a huge variety of disciplines.

Drawing on the aims and methods of several disciplines, Geertz took an interdisciplinary* approach to his work. His theories on culture as systems of meaning had relevance for sociology,* religious studies, psychology, philosophy, and other humanist sciences. They have also intrigued scholars in the disciplines of communication studies, geography, ecology, political science, comparative legal studies,

> ❝ The results suggest that although we can move beyond Geertz, we can never leave him behind. ❞
>
> Jeffrey Alexander et al., *Interpreting Clifford Geertz: Cultural Investigation in the Social Sciences*

history, and literary criticism.[1] His insistence on the distinctiveness of the subjective and contextual* world views of people attracted scholarly attention—as did his interpretive approach to unraveling these world views. Richard Shweder,* another noted American cultural anthropologist, explained that *The Interpretation of Cultures* offers a "provocative" yet "portable" set of beliefs. These have widely appealed to scholars across disciplines.

To many of these scholars Geertz's method remains less important than his cultural pluralism—his way of considering different cultures on their own terms, a notion central to his relativist approach. It also informs his interpretation of alternative moral universes (the idea that there is not an essential human "morality" applicable to all people at all times).[2] Thinkers from other disciplines commonly adapted Geertz's belief "that diversity is inherent to the human condition; that there is no universal essence to human nature." They have also agreed "that the … impulse to value uniformity (convergence in belief) over variety, and to overlook, devalue, or seek to eradicate 'difference,' is not a good thing."[3]

Schools of Thought

By mapping out his particular approach to the analysis of culture, Geertz charted a new direction in anthropological theory and method. He made it contextual and interpretive in nature.[4] In fact, Geertz helped to establish a new school of thought, called "interpretive or symbolic anthropology."* He based this approach to understanding humans and societies on systematically unraveling webs of subjective world views.[5] Interpretive anthropology turned scholars' attention toward issues of culture and interpretation. This may be its most significant accomplishment. Previously, anthropologists had focused almost exclusively on developing grand theories.

Interpretive anthropology arose as a direct reaction to then popular schools of thought such as materialism* and Marxism*—related approaches to understanding history and society that emphasize material factors such as economics and social class. (The materialist school defined culture as consisting only of observable behaviors, while, for Marxists, material factors such as economics and social class are the principle drivers of history.) The school that came to be known as symbolic or interpretive anthropology contributed to the subsequent development of modern schools of thought in the social sciences. It also established how important it is to consider the effect the personality or presence of the researcher has on what he or she investigates.[6]

Other important cultural anthropologists associated with interpretive anthropology include Marshall Sahlins,* David Schneider,* Victor Turner,* and Mary Douglas.* Many consider Geertz and these four prominent scholars as the founders of symbolic or interpretive anthropology.

In Current Scholarship

Clifford Geertz spent the majority of his career doing ethnography* in remote places.[7] He directly supervised only a small number of PhD candidates, but during his 30-year tenure at Princeton's Institute for Advanced Study, Geertz influenced hundreds of social scientists and historians through fellowships, seminars, and lunch conversations.[8]

Whatever discipline they come from, scholars who support and promote *The Interpretation of Cultures* share an affinity for Geertz's interpretivism, his concept of culture, his relativism and particularism* (his belief that every culture should be understood according to the values that it holds, and is a product of its particular historical and environmental context), his intellectual cross-fertilization, and his literary flair. They also appreciate his insistence that we need to understand better the process of understanding.[9] Above all, they feel in harmony with Geertz's call to study human diversity in its plurality.

In their own work Geertz's supporters seem to focus on the issue of making meaning as opposed to the notion of cultural systems.[10] We see this particularly in Geertz's own field of anthropology. Many modern ethnographers continue to study the distinct ways in which people in different localities experience their lives. This group includes Sherry Ortner,* Lila Abu-Lughod,* George Marcus,* and Renato Rosaldo Jr.* Unlike Geertz, however, these practitioners do not view cultures as bounded and isolated. They supplement Geertz's approach by looking at the wider political, economic, social, historical, and cultural frameworks that affect local meaning-making.[11] Geertz's most visible, outspoken, and prominent disciples may be the cultural anthropologists Sherry Ortner, who studied with him, and Richard Shweder.* Both have conducted award-winning academic research.

NOTES

1 See Sherry Ortner, "Special Issue: The Fate of 'Culture': Geertz and beyond," *Representations* 59 (1997): 1–14; and Richard Shweder, "The Resolute Irresolution of Clifford Geertz," *Common Knowledge* 13, nos. 2–3 (Spring–Fall 2007): 191–205.

2 Richard Shweder and Byron Good, eds., *Clifford Geertz by His Colleagues* (Chicago: University of Chicago Press, 2005), 8.

3 Ortner, "Special Issue," 1–14.

4 Sherry Ortner, "Clifford Geertz (1926–2006)," *American Anthropologist* 109, no. 4 (2007), 789.

5 Ortner, "Clifford Geertz (1926–2006)," 787.

6 Ortner, "Clifford Geertz (1926–2006)," 787.

7 Ortner, "Clifford Geertz (1926–2006)," 788.

8   Ortner, "Clifford Geertz (1926–2006)," 787.

9   Shweder and Good, *Clifford Geertz by His Colleagues,* 9.

10   Ortner, "Special Issue," 1.

11   Ortner, "Special Issue," 1–14.

MODULE 11
IMPACT AND INFLUENCE TODAY

KEY POINTS

- *The Interpretation of Cultures* is one of a body of revered works for anthropologists practicing interpretive* scholarship.

- Although these scholars have widely adopted Geertz's "interpretive turn," the general consensus remains that anthropologists need to supplement the Geertzian concept of culture for it to be relevant in the modern world.

- Following Geertz, anthropologists need to reconfigure the concept of culture for an increasingly interdependent, complex, and ever-changing world.

Position

Some 40 years after its initial publication, Clifford Geertz's *The Interpretation of Cultures* has become part of a "sacred canon."[1] Today, it forms part of the essential reading list for anyone interested in interpretive approaches in the social sciences and humanities.

Scholars generally agree that they need to complement the Geertzian concept of culture with additional research looking at wider political, economic, social, and historical conditions. But the relevance of *The Interpretation of Cultures* has not diminished.[2] The discipline has widely adopted Geertz's so-called "interpretive turn." To this day it remains the approach taken by many cultural and social anthropologists.* Historians, sociologists,* political scientists, and scholars of other disciplines who collect ethnographic* data in their research projects also use Geertz's approach.[3] They share with him the interpretive method of teasing out and analyzing the meanings of

> ❝ Whatever the infirmities of the concept of 'culture' [...] are, there is nothing for it but to persist in spite of them. ❞
>
> Sherry Ortner, *Special Issue: The Fate of 'Culture': Geertz and beyond*

texts and performances.

In the same vein, they also share with Geertz an affinity for cultural relativism*—the need to understand other societies through the values those societies hold. In the age of globalization—the trend toward increasingly close cultural, economic, and political ties across continental boundaries—*The Interpretation of Cultures* continues to help us understand difference, in particular "different conceptions of the self, of morality, of emotions, of religions, of political authority, of kinship, of time, as made manifest by groups of people, ways of life."[4] *The Interpretation of Cultures* remains widely debated and cited inside and outside of anthropology.

Interaction

Interpretive scholars across disciplines endorse Geertz's insistence on understanding meaning. They respect him as a brilliant "cultural theorist, an ethnographer, and a moral philosopher."[5]

Still, the Geertzian concept of culture has given rise to passionate debates among interpretive scholars. They argue that Geertz's classic definition of what culture is has proven less and less relevant to the modern world.[6] These scholars note that today's world contains fewer distinct and recognizable cultures and fewer coherent ways of life. Scholars also find beliefs, practices, and feelings have become less unified even within a family unit, not to mention the larger groupings of tribe, community, nation, or civilization.[7] They also agree that culture appears in new fluid and complex social formations today. The characteristics of the modern "tribes" formed by global networks, social media communities, and mixed identities include globalization, complexity, and vastness.[8] Current social and political phenomena seriously call into question the usefulness of Geertz's concept of culture as unified, static, and uncontaminated by outside forces.

As a result, scholars have devoted a considerable amount of time to research rethinking and modernizing the notion of cultural systems.[9] Like Geertz, many modern ethnographers continue to study the distinct ways in which people in different localities experience their lives. Unlike Geertz, they do not view cultures as bounded and isolated. If they supplement the Geertzian approach they do so by looking at wider political, economic, social, historical, and cultural frameworks that affect local cultures and their interplay with power.[10]

The Continuing Debate

Renowned present-day cultural anthropologists such as Sherry Ortner,* Lila Abu-Lughod,* George Marcus,* or Renato Rosaldo Jr.* have discussed a variety of practical responses to the "profound and far-reaching" critiques of Geertz's concept of culture.[11] Key topics in the debate include the reconfiguration of anthropology's core concept of culture and the realities for ethnography* in the face of globalization. They have also reexamined practical forms of modern anthropological fieldwork.[12]

The influential contemporary cultural anthropologist Sherry Ortner studied with Geertz. She has produced useful summaries of the ongoing debate and reflected on a productive way forward.[13] Ortner argues that the issue should not be whether to banish or to hold on to a Geertzian concept of culture, and by extension, the classic "anthropological project."[14] She makes the extremely valid point that "the issue is, once again, one of reconfiguring this enormously productive concept for a changing world, a changing relationship between politics and academic life, and a changing landscape of theoretical possibilities."[15]

Ortner suggests three imperatives for rethinking culture.[16] First, she proposes "to maintain a strong presumption of cultural difference, but make it do new kinds of work." [17]Second, Ortner argues that modern thinkers should focus on the issue of making meaning in *The Interpretation of Cultures*, rather than the notion of cultural systems. And third, she claims that scholars should situate their cultural analysis "within and, as it were, beneath larger analyses of social and political events and processes" because "cultural analysis can no longer … be an end in itself."[18] In other words, she calls on scholars to value the "meaning-laden" and "meaning-making" aspects of the Geertzian view. But she recognizes that they must seek to locate (in the sense of "detect" or "identify") and examine culture in new and different ways.

NOTES

1   Pauline Turner Strong, "Book Review Essays: Anthropology and the Future of (Inter) Disciplinarity," *American Anthropologist* 110, no. 2 (June 2008): 253.

2   Sherry Ortner, "Special Issue: The Fate of 'Culture': Geertz and beyond," *Representations* 59 (1997), 1–14.

3   Ortner, "Special Issue," 6.

4   Richard Shweder, "The Resolute Irresolution of Clifford Geertz," *Common Knowledge* 13, nos. 2–3 (Spring 2007), 203.

5   Ortner, "Special Issue," 2.

6   Ortner, "Special Issue," 7.

7   Ortner, "Special Issue," 7.

8   Ortner, "Special Issue," 7–8.

9   Ortner, "Special Issue," 1.

10 Ortner, "Special Issue," 7–8.

11 Ortner, "Special Issue," 8.

12 Ortner, "Special Issue," 7–9.

13 Ortner, "Special Issue," 1–14.

14 Ortner, "Special Issue," 1–14.

15 Ortner, "Special Issue," 8.

16 Ortner, "Special Issue," 8.

17 Ortner, "Special Issue," 8.

18 Ortner, "Special Issue," 9.

MODULE 12
WHERE NEXT?

KEY POINTS

- *The Interpretation of Cultures* will continue to be remembered as a classic work valuing the aspects of social life associated with the production and the transmission of meaning.

- This seminal work continues to be useful in addressing "issues of social and moral philosophy." That usefulness seems unlikely to diminish.

- In *The Interpretation of Cultures* Geertz set out to establish what culture is and how it should be studied, introducing the concept of thick description—the detailed, interpretive analysis of human behavior in context.

Potential

Scholars will continue to remember Clifford Geertz's *The Interpretation of Cultures* as a classic, and Geertz himself has been credited with "reconfiguring, almost single-handedly, the boundary between the social sciences and the humanities for the second half of the twentieth century."[1] While much about the world has changed since Geertz wrote the book, this work will continue to serve as a key reference for a larger, ongoing debate about culture. Geertz's central proposition has a timeless quality and universal applicability. As his student Sherry Ortner* wrote, he wanted to understand the human condition "as defined by the constant production and transformation of meaning."[2] Geertz proposed the idea that every material, political, social, or intimate aspect of human existence is "at the same time culturally defined, shaped, and laden with cognitive and affective meaning." Scholars will likely continue to see the ripple effect of this notion

> " Culture, if it is to continue to be understood as a vital part of the social process, must be located and examined in very different ways: as the clash of meanings in borderlands; as public culture that has its own textual coherence but is always locally interpreted; as fragile webs of story and meaning woven by vulnerable actors in nightmarish situations; as the grounds of agency and intentionality in ongoing social practice. "
>
> Sherry Ortner, *Special Issue: The Fate of 'Culture': Geertz and beyond*

across academic disciplines for the foreseeable future.[3]

Still, some scholars have pointed out deficits in the work. They note that *The Interpretation of Cultures* neglects issues of power, conflict, and inequality.[4] Critics have said it is not politically progressive, too ethically neutral, too invested in a certain concept of culture, and too descriptive where it should be explanatory.[5] Still, scholars assert that *The Interpretation of Cultures* has important implications for the politics of anthropology as a science as well as the politics within the field of anthropology. These will remain relevant in the future.[6] The work's theoretical usefulness in addressing "issues of social and moral philosophy" also remains unlikely to diminish.[7]

For that reason, Ortner proposes that when we value the "meaning-laden" and "meaning-making" aspects of social life (those parts of social life to do with the transmission or production of meaning), we continue to assume a "fundamentally Geertzian view."[8]

Future Directions

Future uses for this work will almost certainly be characterized by anthropological self-questioning. We will likely see further attempts to upgrade the Geertzian concept of culture. Scholars may also attempt to reconfigure his understanding of anthropology in relation to the multidimensional social formations that have emerged since Geertz wrote this work. These complex formations include nations, transnational networks, changing discourses (the systems of language and assumptions that we draw on when the think or talk about certain subjects), global "flows" (the movement of goods, people, ideas, technology, and so on), increasingly mixed identities, social media groups, and so forth.

Ortner sums up the overarching questions that will guide future scholars: "How can anthropology hold on to ethnographic* work in the deepest sense—long-term, intense, linguistically competent, whole-self, participant observation*—in a world of these kinds of forms and processes? What kinds of relationship(s) can/may/should obtain between the resolute localness and face-to-faceness of ethnographic work and the vastness, complexity, and especially non-localness of such formations?"[9]

Some recent cultural scholars do not see their work as engaging with the Geertzian perspective. In fact, they do not consider that they engage with cultural anthropology at all. But modern cultural anthropologists such as Sherry Ortner, Renato Rosaldo Jr.,* and Lila Abu-Lughod* point toward a direction that welcomes "the ethnographies and histories of zones of friction between cultures, in which the clash of power and meaning and identities is the stuff of change and transformation."[10] For example, Ortner wrote a book examining the history of encounters in Himalayan mountaineering.[11] On the one side, she discusses Western mountaineers. These men appear rather "savage" in her account. For one thing, they insist on slaughtering animals for meat during their expeditions. On the other side she finds Buddhist Sherpas*—inhabitants of the region around Mount Everest. These men have a profound aversion to killing, although they are not exactly nonviolent themselves.

Summary

In *The Interpretation of Cultures*, Clifford Geertz took on the intellectual challenge of identifying "what culture is, what role it plays in social life, and how it ought properly to be studied."[12] Geertz's particular approach to the study of culture centered on unraveling the webs of subjectively held meaning that groups of people share. Geertz examined the symbols of a culture and found that they embody systems of meanings.[13]

Above all, the seminal text contributed to an emerging trend of modern cultural anthropology in the twentieth-century United States. Geertz helped his peers focus how people see themselves and the world in which they live. He paid special attention to symbols such as crafts and myths. Most famously, *The Interpretation of Cultures* introduced the notion of thick description. Geertz used this interpretive process to explain the shared meaning that specific symbolic acts hold for the individuals whose actions they are. Thick description facilitates his attempts to state "what the knowledge thus attained demonstrates about the society in which it is found and, beyond that, about social life as such."[14] For many inside and outside the field, thick description came to explain not only what Geertz did but also what cultural anthropologists in general do.[15] Thick description focused on meaning-making—the way that actions come to acquire symbolic weight—and interpretation. This brought cultural anthropology closer to the humanities than the natural sciences. With his peers Marshall Sahlins,* David Schneider,* Victor Turner,* and Mary Douglas,* Geertz became known as a major voice of the 1960s "symbolic"* or "interpretive"* school of thought.

NOTES

1 Sherry Ortner, "Special Issue: The Fate of 'Culture': Geertz and beyond," *Representations* 59 (1997): 1.

2   Sherry Ortner, "Clifford Geertz (1926–2006)," *American Anthropologist* 109, no. 4 (2007), 786.

3   Ortner, "Clifford Geertz (1926–2006)," 787.

4   Edward Bruner, "Book Review: Clifford Geertz: His Critics and Followers, 1998," *Anthropology and Humanism* 23, no. 2 (1998): 216.

5   Aram Yengoyan, "Clifford Geertz, Cultural Portraits, and Southeast Asia," *The Journal of Asian Studies* 68, no. 4 (November 2009): 1217.

6   Ortner, "Special Issue," 4.

7   Ortner, "Special Issue," 5.

8   Ortner, "Special Issue," 11.

9   Ortner, "Special Issue," 7–8.

10 Ortner, "Special Issue," 8.

11 Sherry Ortner, *Life and Death on Mt. Everest: Sherpas and Himalayan Mountaineering* (Princeton: Princeton University Press, 1999).

12 Clifford Geertz, *The Interpretation of Cultures*, 2nd edn (New York: Basic Books, 2000), vii.

13 Geertz, *The Interpretation of Cultures*, 125.

14 Geertz, *The Interpretation of Cultures*, 26–7.

15 Ortner, "Clifford Geertz (1926–2006)," 787.

GLOSSARY

GLOSSARY OF TERMS

Anti-Semitism: discrimination against or prejudice or hostility toward Jews.

Archaeological anthropology: the study of the origin, growth, and development of human culture from the distant past.

Biological anthropology: the study of how the human species evolved.

Buddhist Sherpas: people who inhabit the regions surrounding Mount Everest and adhere to the religious traditions of Tibetan Buddhism.

Cognitive anthropology: the branch of anthropology that examines how what people know shapes the way they perceive their surroundings and relate to the world.

Cold War: a period of tension from 1947 to 1991 between the United States and its Western allies and the Eastern federation of countries known as the Soviet Union.

Colonialism: the practice of forcibly gaining control over another country, populating it with nonnative settlers, and appropriating its resources and assets.

Contextual: based on the circumstances and context.

Cultural anthropology: the branch of anthropology that looks at the roots, history, and development of human culture.

Culture: according to Geertz, a system of shared meaning that ought to be studied by interpreting the symbols of that culture, such as art and myths.

Cyberbullying: practice common among young people in Western societies of isolating and picking on members of their peer group via online interactions using computers and mobile phones.

Ecological anthropology: a discipline studying the relationship between humans and their biophysical environment.

Empyrean: of or relating to heaven.

Ethnography: research that explores cultural phenomena and documents its findings in written field studies or case studies.

Functionalism: a viewpoint analyzing society in terms of how its elements function.

Global warming: a rise in temperatures in the Earth's atmosphere with potentially very serious effects and caused in part by an increase in atmospheric greenhouse gases due to human activity.

Historical particularism: a belief that every society is the product of its particular historical journey.

Holistic: the belief that the parts of something are intimately interconnected and explicable only by reference to the whole.

Iklas: the Javanese concept of a detached acceptance of death.

Indonesia: an archipelago of thousands of islands in southeast Asia organized as a sovereign state, the Republic of Indonesia.

Interdisciplinary: research that draws on the aims and methods of several different academic disciplines.

Interpretive approach or interpretivism: in anthropology, an approach that believes that anthropologists should understand how peoples and cultures see themselves, and then translate the cultural meanings to outsiders.

Linguistic anthropology: the study of language as it represents culture.

Marxism: a socioeconomic and political world view developed in the nineteenth century by the German political philosopher Karl Marx, based on his propositions of how capitalism developed and shaped the struggle of the classes.

Materialism: a view that holds that nothing exists except matter, and therefore things can only be measured or known through the senses.

Natural science: a branch of science that seeks to describe, predict, and understand natural phenomena and reveal the "laws of nature."

Participant observation: a data-collection method by which researchers live among the people they study, observe them, and participate in their social life.

Particularism: the exclusive attachment to one's own interest, group, party, or nation.

Positivism: a standpoint that rejects introspective and intuitive knowledge. Positivists believe that only logical and mathematical methods are scientific and trustworthy enough in uncovering the laws of society.

Postcolonialism: an intellectual direction (sometimes also referred to as an "era" or "theory") that arose around the middle of the twentieth century when formerly colonized countries became independent. As an intellectual approach, postcolonial studies analyzes the various cultural, linguistic, and social legacies of the colonial period.

Relativism: the concept that points of view have no absolute truth or validity, but only relative, subjective value according to how different people perceive and consider them.

Rendition: a performance or interpretation, especially of a dramatic role or piece of music.

Rukun: the Javanese concept of communal harmony.

Semiotics: the study of signs and sign systems, both linguistic and nonlinguistic, in relation to the way they are transmitted.

Social anthropology: the study of social structures and their role in human cultures.

Social revolution: a revolution by the people (rather than, say, political parties) that aims to reorganize society, such as the civil rights movements in the United States in 1954–68.

Sociology: the study of social behavior, social institutions, and the origins and organization of human society.

Structuralism: the theory that we must understand elements of human culture in terms of their relationship to a larger, overarching system or structure.

Subjectivity: the notion that a person's perspective is shaped by his or her personal and unique feelings, experiences, beliefs, and desires.

Symbolic anthropology: the branch of anthropology that views culture as a set of symbolic systems, and studies rituals and symbols to unpick their cultural meanings.

Thick description: a description that explains not just a particular human behavior, but also its context, in a way that makes the behavior meaningful to an outsider.

Verstehen: German word meaning the emphatic understanding of human behavior.

Virtual friends: people known via online interactions on social networking services, message boards, shared-interest websites, and so on.

World War II (1939–45): a global conflict between the Axis Powers (Germany, Italy, and Japan) and the ultimately victorious Allied Powers (the United Kingdom and its colonies, the Soviet Union, and the United States)

PEOPLE MENTIONED IN THE TEXT

Lila Abu-Lughod (b. 1952) is an American anthropologist with Palestinian and Jewish ancestry. Her research interests focus on nationalism, media, gender politics, and the politics of memory. She wrote the much-reprinted article "Do Muslim Women Really Need Saving?" (2002).

Talal Asad (b. 1932) is an anthropologist who is known for his writings on postcolonialism, Christianity, Islam, and ritual studies.

Jane Austen (1775–1817) was an English novelist. She is the author of *Sense and Sensibility* (1811), *Pride and Prejudice* (1813), and *Emma* (1815), among other novels.

Karen Blu (b. 1941) is emerita anthropology professor at New York University. She is well known for her research on the American Indian people.

Franz Boas (1858–1942) was the founder of modern American anthropology. He established the concept of cultural relativity, and argued that all humans have the same intellectual capacity. In 1920, he wrote the programmatic essay "The Methods of Ethnology."

Pierre Bourdieu (1930–2002) was a French sociologist, philosopher, and anthropologist. Bourdieu published some 30 books and more than 300 articles on an astounding variety of topics. His empirically rich yet theoretically dense style can deter some readers.

Mary Douglas (1921–2007) was a British anthropologist. Her group/grid pattern laid the foundation for cultural theory, and her work on risk analysis pioneered economic anthropology. Her best-known book remains *Purity and Danger: An Analysis of Concepts of Pollution and Taboo*, first published in 1966.

Louis Dumont (1911–98) was a French anthropologist specializing in India. He is best known to anthropologists for his work on Indian caste and kinship.

Émile Durkheim (1858–1917) was a French sociologist, psychologist, and philosopher. Together with the political philosopher Karl Marx and the sociologist Max Weber, Durkheim is famous for founding modern sociology. He is best known for his book *Suicide* (1897), an exploration of suicides in different populations.

Charles Frake (b. 1930) was a linguistic anthropologist of the twentieth century. In 1969 he published "The Ethnographic Study of Cognitive Systems."

Sigmund Freud (1856–1939) was an Austrian neurologist, now known as the founder of modern psychoanalysis.

Hildred Storey Geertz (b. 1929) is professor emeritus of anthropology at Princeton University, where she delivers classes on the history of anthropological theory, the anthropology of art, and the art of ethnography. She has conducted fieldwork in Java, Morocco, and Bali.

George R. Geiger (1903–98) was a professor of philosophy at Antioch College. He joined the faculty in 1937 on the recommendation of the noted philosopher John Dewey and continued teaching part time even after his formal retirement in 1969. He became one of the most famous "interpreters" of the philosophy of Henry George.

Marvin Harris (1927–2001) was an American anthropologist influential in the development of cultural materialism. He wrote the defining work *The Rise of Anthropological Theory: A History of Theories of Culture.*

Roger Keesing (1935–93) was an anthropologist who is best known for his research on the Kwaio people of Malaita in the Solomon Islands. His studies are concerned with kinship, religion, politics, and language.

Clyde Kluckhohn (1905–60) was a professor in social anthropology and social relations at Harvard University. He is best known for studying the language and culture of the Navajo, and for developing a methodological approach called the Values Orientation Theory.

Claude Lévi-Strauss (1908–2009) was a French social anthropologist and is associated with founding and advocating structuralism, which analyzes the structures of cultural systems such as kinship.

George Marcus (b. 1968) is an American cultural anthropologist with a research interest in power and its effects on ordinary people. Marcus also founded the journal *Cultural Anthropology* in 1986.

Bronisław Malinowski (1884–1942) was one of the most influential anthropologists of the twentieth century. He is known for founding social anthropology and conducted most of his research on the peoples of Oceania.

Karl Marx (1818–83) was a philosopher, sociologist, and economist. Most people know him for being a revolutionary communist because his writings were the foundation for many communist regimes in the twentieth century. His main work is *Das Kapital* ("Capital"), published in three volumes in 1867–94.

C. Wright Mills (1916–62) was an American sociologist, who worked at Columbia University from 1946 until his death. His best-known publications include *White Collar* (1951), *The Power Elite* (1956), and *The Sociological Imagination* (1959).

Sherry Ortner (b. 1941) is a cultural anthropologist who studied with Geertz and is best known for her theories on transformation and resistance.

Talcott Parsons (1902–79) is widely considered one of the twentieth century's most influential American sociologists. He was responsible for introducing the pioneering sociologist Max Weber to American scholarship, and also argued for a focus on people's subjective realities. His major works included *The Structure of Social Action* (1937) and *The Social System* (1951).

Alfred Radcliffe-Brown (1881–1955) was an English social anthropologist. His work was concerned with how the social structures of preindustrial societies functioned. On this basis, he developed his theory of functionalism.

Roy Rappaport (1926–97) was an anthropologist who particularly contributed to the study of rituals and ecological anthropology.

Richard Rorty (1931–2007) was an influential, pragmatic American philosopher. His major works included *Philosophy and the Mirror of Nature* (1979).

Renato Rosaldo Jr. (b. 1941) is one of the world's leading cultural anthropologists, with a particular interest in cultural citizenship.

Gilbert Ryle (1900–76) was an English philosopher concerned with the nature and use of language. Principally known for asserting that the workings of the mind remain connected to the actions of the body, he is best known for his book *The Concept of Mind* (1949).

Marshall Sahlins (b. 1930) is an anthropologist at the University of Chicago. His work focuses on the power of culture in shaping people's perceptions and actions.

Ferdinand de Saussure (1857–1913) was a Swiss linguist who is considered a founding father of modern linguistics and the study of meaning-making or signification. He is best known for his posthumously published lectures on linguistics.

David M. Schneider (1918–95) was a major proponent of the symbolic anthropological approach, and is particularly known for his studies on kinship.

Richard Shweder (b. 1945) is an American cultural anthropologist who wrote *Thinking through Cultures: Expeditions in Cultural Psychology* (1991) and *Why Do Men Barbecue? Recipes for Cultural Psychology* (2003).

James Spradley (1933–82) was a prolific American anthropologist who believed that researchers should look for the meaning that participants make of their lives.

Victor Turner (1920–83) was a Scottish anthropologist who is famous for his research on rituals and rites of passage.

Edward Burnett Tylor (1832–1917) was an English anthropologist who is credited with founding cultural anthropology. His most influential work remains *Primitive Culture* (1871).

Andrew P.Vayda (b. 1931) is an ecological anthropologist, specializing in methodology and explanation. He primarily explores the interface between social and ecological science in Indonesia and Papua New Guinea.

Max Weber (1864–1920) was a German sociologist. Scholars consider him one of the three founding architects of sociology, along with the French social theorist Émile Durkheim and the German political philosopher Karl Marx. He is known for his ideas on bureaucracy and his most influential essay "The Protestant Ethic and the Spirit of Capitalism" (1934).

Aram Yengoyan (b. 1936) is an American professor in anthropology with particular expertise in Southeast Asia.

WORKS CITED

WORKS CITED

Alexander, Jeffrey, Philip Smith, Matthew Norton, and Peter Brooks, eds. *Interpreting Clifford Geertz: Cultural Investigation in the Social Sciences.* New York: Palgrave Macmillan, 2011.

Asad, Talal. "Anthropological Conceptions of Religion: Reflections on Geertz." *Man* 18, no. 2 (1983): 237–59.

Bourdieu, Pierre. *Distinction: A Social Critique of the Judgement of Taste.* Translated by Richard Nice. Cambridge, MA: Harvard University Press, 1987.

Bruner, Edward. "Book Review: Clifford Geertz: His Critics and Followers, 1998." *Anthropology and Humanism* 23, no. 2 (1998): 215–16.

Geertz, Clifford. *After the Fact: Two Countries, Four Decades, One Anthropologist.* Cambridge, MA: Harvard University Press, 1995.

———. *Agricultural Involution: The Processes of Ecological Change in Indonesia.* Los Angeles: University of California Press, 1963.

———. *Available Light: Anthropological Reflections on Philosophical Topics.* Princeton: Princeton University Press, 2000.

———. *The Interpretation of Cultures.* 2nd edn. New York: Basic Books, 2000.

———. *Islam Observed: Religious Development in Morocco and Indonesia.* New Haven: Yale University Press, 1968.

———. *Kinship in Bali.* Chicago: University of Chicago Press, 1975.

———. *Life among the Anthros and Other Essays.* Princeton: Princeton University Press, 2010.

———. *Local Knowledge: Further Essays in Interpretive Anthropology.* New York: Basic Books, 1983.

———. "Passage and Accident: A Life of Learning." In *Available Light: Anthropological Reflections on Philosophical Topics*, by Clifford Geertz. Princeton: Princeton University Press, 2000.

———. *Peddlers and Princes: Social Development and Economic Change in Two Indonesian Towns.* Chicago: University of Chicago Press, 1963.

———. *Person, Time, and Conduct in Bali: An Essay in Cultural Analysis.* New Haven: Yale University Southeast Asia Studies, 1966.

———. *The Religion of Java.* Glencoe: The Free Press, *1960*.

———. *Works and Lives: The Anthropologist as Author.* Stanford: Stanford

University Press, 1988.

Geertz, Clifford, ed. *Myth, Symbol, and Culture.* New York: Norton, 1971.

Geertz, Clifford, Hildred Geertz, and Lawrence Rosen. *Meaning and Order in Moroccan Society.* New York: Cambridge University Press, 1979.

Institute for Advanced Study. "Clifford Geertz 1926–2006." Accessed December 8, 2015. https://www.ias.edu/news/press-releases/2009-49

Keesing, Roger. "Theories of Culture." *Annual Review of Anthropology* 3 (1974): 73–97.

Kronenfeld, David, Giovanni Bennardo, Victor de Munck, and Michael Fischer, eds. *A Companion to Cognitive Anthropology*. Singapore: Blackwell Publishing Ltd., 2011.

Leopold, Joan. *Culture in Comparative and Evolutionary Perspective: E. B. Tylor and the Making of Primitive Culture.* Berlin: Dietrich Reimer Verlag, 1980.

Lévi-Strauss, Claude. *The Savage Mind*. Chicago: University of Chicago Press, 1966.

Lewis, Diane. "Anthropology and Colonialism." *Current Anthropology* 14, no. 5 (December 1973): 581–602.

Mills, C. Wright. *The Sociological Imagination*. New York: Oxford University Press, 1959.

Ortner, Sherry. "Clifford Geertz (1926–2006)." *American Anthropologist* 109, no. 4 (2007): 786–98.

— — —. *Life and Death on Mt. Everest: Sherpas and Himalayan Mountaineering.* Princeton: Princeton University Press, 1999.

— — —. "Special Issue: The Fate of 'Culture': Geertz and beyond." *Representations* 59 (1997): 1–14.

Parsons, Talcott. *The Social System*. New York: Free Press, 1951.

Rosaldo, Renato Jr. "Geertz's Gifts." *Common Knowledge* 13, nos. 2–3 (2007).

Ryle, Gilbert. *The Concept of Mind*. Chicago: University of Chicago Press, 1949.

Sahlins, Marshall. *Culture and Practical Reason.* Chicago: University of Chicago Press, 1978.

Schneider, David. *American Kinship: A Cultural Account*. 2nd edn. Chicago: University of Chicago Press, 1980.

Shweder, Richard. "Clifford Geertz." *Proceedings of the American Philosophical Society* 154, no. 1 (March 2010): 87–93.

———. *Clifford James Geertz: 1926–2006, A Biographical Memoir*. Washington, DC: National Academy of Sciences. Accessed November 2, 2015. https://www.sss.ias.edu/files/pdfs/Geertz_NAS_6-10-10.pdf.

———. "The Resolute Irresolution of Clifford Geertz." *Common Knowledge* 13, nos. 2–3 (Spring–Fall 2007): 191–205.

Shweder, Richard, and Byron Good, eds. *Clifford Geertz by His Colleagues*. Chicago: University of Chicago Press, 2005.

Turner Strong, Pauline. "Book Review Essays: Anthropology and the Future of (Inter) Disciplinarity." *American Anthropologist* 110, no. 2 (June 2008): 253.

Tylor, Edward Burnett. *Primitive Culture: Researches into the Development of Mythology, Philosophy, Religion, Language, Art and Custom*. 2 vols. London: John Murray 1871.

Weber, Max. *The Protestant Ethic and the Spirit of Capitalism*. Translated by Talcott Parsons. London, New York: Routledge, 2001.

Yarrow, Andrew. "Clifford Geertz, Cultural Anthropologist, Is Dead at 80." *New York Times*, November 1, 2006. Accessed December 8, 2015. http://www.nytimes.com/2006/11/01/obituaries/01geertz.html?pagewanted=print&_r=0

Yengoyan, Aram. "Clifford Geertz, Cultural Portraits, and Southeast Asia." *The Journal of Asian Studies* 68, no. 4 (November 2009): 1215–30.

THE MACAT LIBRARY
BY DISCIPLINE

The Macat Library By Discipline

AFRICANA STUDIES

Chinua Achebe's *An Image of Africa: Racism in Conrad's Heart of Darkness*
W. E. B. Du Bois's *The Souls of Black Folk*
Zora Neale Huston's *Characteristics of Negro Expression*
Martin Luther King Jr's *Why We Can't Wait*
Toni Morrison's *Playing in the Dark: Whiteness in the American Literary Imagination*

ANTHROPOLOGY

Arjun Appadurai's *Modernity at Large: Cultural Dimensions of Globalisation*
Philippe Ariès's *Centuries of Childhood*
Franz Boas's *Race, Language and Culture*
Kim Chan & Renée Mauborgne's *Blue Ocean Strategy*
Jared Diamond's *Guns, Germs & Steel: the Fate of Human Societies*
Jared Diamond's *Collapse: How Societies Choose to Fail or Survive*
E. E. Evans-Pritchard's *Witchcraft, Oracles and Magic Among the Azande*
James Ferguson's *The Anti-Politics Machine*
Clifford Geertz's *The Interpretation of Cultures*
David Graeber's *Debt: the First 5000 Years*
Karen Ho's *Liquidated: An Ethnography of Wall Street*
Geert Hofstede's *Culture's Consequences: Comparing Values, Behaviors, Institutes and Organizations across Nations*
Claude Lévi-Strauss's *Structural Anthropology*
Jay Macleod's *Ain't No Makin' It: Aspirations and Attainment in a Low-Income Neighborhood*
Saba Mahmood's *The Politics of Piety: The Islamic Revival and the Feminist Subject*
Marcel Mauss's *The Gift*

BUSINESS

Jean Lave & Etienne Wenger's *Situated Learning*
Theodore Levitt's *Marketing Myopia*
Burton G. Malkiel's *A Random Walk Down Wall Street*
Douglas McGregor's *The Human Side of Enterprise*
Michael Porter's *Competitive Strategy: Creating and Sustaining Superior Performance*
John Kotter's *Leading Change*
C. K. Prahalad & Gary Hamel's *The Core Competence of the Corporation*

CRIMINOLOGY

Michelle Alexander's *The New Jim Crow: Mass Incarceration in the Age of Colorblindness*
Michael R. Gottfredson & Travis Hirschi's *A General Theory of Crime*
Richard Herrnstein & Charles A. Murray's *The Bell Curve: Intelligence and Class Structure in American Life*
Elizabeth Loftus's *Eyewitness Testimony*
Jay Macleod's *Ain't No Makin' It: Aspirations and Attainment in a Low-Income Neighborhood*
Philip Zimbardo's *The Lucifer Effect*

ECONOMICS

Janet Abu-Lughod's *Before European Hegemony*
Ha-Joon Chang's *Kicking Away the Ladder*
David Brion Davis's *The Problem of Slavery in the Age of Revolution*
Milton Friedman's *The Role of Monetary Policy*
Milton Friedman's *Capitalism and Freedom*
David Graeber's *Debt: the First 5000 Years*
Friedrich Hayek's *The Road to Serfdom*
Karen Ho's *Liquidated: An Ethnography of Wall Street*

John Maynard Keynes's *The General Theory of Employment, Interest and Money*
Charles P. Kindleberger's *Manias, Panics and Crashes*
Robert Lucas's *Why Doesn't Capital Flow from Rich to Poor Countries?*
Burton G. Malkiel's *A Random Walk Down Wall Street*
Thomas Robert Malthus's *An Essay on the Principle of Population*
Karl Marx's *Capital*
Thomas Piketty's *Capital in the Twenty-First Century*
Amartya Sen's *Development as Freedom*
Adam Smith's *The Wealth of Nations*
Nassim Nicholas Taleb's *The Black Swan: The Impact of the Highly Improbable*
Amos Tversky's & Daniel Kahneman's *Judgment under Uncertainty: Heuristics and Biases*
Mahbub Ul Haq's *Reflections on Human Development*
Max Weber's *The Protestant Ethic and the Spirit of Capitalism*

FEMINISM AND GENDER STUDIES

Judith Butler's *Gender Trouble*
Simone De Beauvoir's *The Second Sex*
Michel Foucault's *History of Sexuality*
Betty Friedan's *The Feminine Mystique*
Saba Mahmood's *The Politics of Piety: The Islamic Revival and the Feminist Subject*
Joan Wallach Scott's *Gender and the Politics of History*
Mary Wollstonecraft's *A Vindication of the Rights of Woman*
Virginia Woolf's *A Room of One's Own*

GEOGRAPHY

The Brundtland Report's *Our Common Future*
Rachel Carson's *Silent Spring*
Charles Darwin's *On the Origin of Species*
James Ferguson's *The Anti-Politics Machine*
Jane Jacobs's *The Death and Life of Great American Cities*
James Lovelock's *Gaia: A New Look at Life on Earth*
Amartya Sen's *Development as Freedom*
Mathis Wackernagel & William Rees's *Our Ecological Footprint*

HISTORY

Janet Abu-Lughod's *Before European Hegemony*
Benedict Anderson's *Imagined Communities*
Bernard Bailyn's *The Ideological Origins of the American Revolution*
Hanna Batatu's *The Old Social Classes And The Revolutionary Movements Of Iraq*
Christopher Browning's *Ordinary Men: Reserve Police Batallion 101 and the Final Solution in Poland*
Edmund Burke's *Reflections on the Revolution in France*
William Cronon's *Nature's Metropolis: Chicago And The Great West*
Alfred W. Crosby's *The Columbian Exchange*
Hamid Dabashi's *Iran: A People Interrupted*
David Brion Davis's *The Problem of Slavery in the Age of Revolution*
Nathalie Zemon Davis's *The Return of Martin Guerre*
Jared Diamond's *Guns, Germs & Steel: the Fate of Human Societies*
Frank Dikotter's *Mao's Great Famine*
John W Dower's *War Without Mercy: Race And Power In The Pacific War*
W. E. B. Du Bois's *The Souls of Black Folk*
Richard J. Evans's *In Defence of History*
Lucien Febvre's *The Problem of Unbelief in the 16th Century*
Sheila Fitzpatrick's *Everyday Stalinism*

The Macat Library By Discipline

Eric Foner's *Reconstruction: America's Unfinished Revolution, 1863-1877*
Michel Foucault's *Discipline and Punish*
Michel Foucault's *History of Sexuality*
Francis Fukuyama's *The End of History and the Last Man*
John Lewis Gaddis's *We Now Know: Rethinking Cold War History*
Ernest Gellner's *Nations and Nationalism*
Eugene Genovese's *Roll, Jordan, Roll: The World the Slaves Made*
Carlo Ginzburg's *The Night Battles*
Daniel Goldhagen's *Hitler's Willing Executioners*
Jack Goldstone's *Revolution and Rebellion in the Early Modern World*
Antonio Gramsci's *The Prison Notebooks*
Alexander Hamilton, John Jay & James Madison's *The Federalist Papers*
Christopher Hill's *The World Turned Upside Down*
Carole Hillenbrand's *The Crusades: Islamic Perspectives*
Thomas Hobbes's *Leviathan*
Eric Hobsbawm's *The Age Of Revolution*
John A. Hobson's *Imperialism: A Study*
Albert Hourani's *History of the Arab Peoples*
Samuel P. Huntington's *The Clash of Civilizations and the Remaking of World Order*
C. L. R. James's *The Black Jacobins*
Tony Judt's *Postwar: A History of Europe Since 1945*
Ernst Kantorowicz's *The King's Two Bodies: A Study in Medieval Political Theology*
Paul Kennedy's *The Rise and Fall of the Great Powers*
Ian Kershaw's *The "Hitler Myth": Image and Reality in the Third Reich*
John Maynard Keynes's *The General Theory of Employment, Interest and Money*
Charles P. Kindleberger's *Manias, Panics and Crashes*
Martin Luther King Jr's *Why We Can't Wait*
Henry Kissinger's *World Order: Reflections on the Character of Nations and the Course of History*
Thomas Kuhn's *The Structure of Scientific Revolutions*
Georges Lefebvre's *The Coming of the French Revolution*
John Locke's *Two Treatises of Government*
Niccolò Machiavelli's *The Prince*
Thomas Robert Malthus's *An Essay on the Principle of Population*
Mahmood Mamdani's *Citizen and Subject: Contemporary Africa And The Legacy Of Late Colonialism*
Karl Marx's *Capital*
Stanley Milgram's *Obedience to Authority*
John Stuart Mill's *On Liberty*
Thomas Paine's *Common Sense*
Thomas Paine's *Rights of Man*
Geoffrey Parker's *Global Crisis: War, Climate Change and Catastrophe in the Seventeenth Century*
Jonathan Riley-Smith's *The First Crusade and the Idea of Crusading*
Jean-Jacques Rousseau's *The Social Contract*
Joan Wallach Scott's *Gender and the Politics of History*
Theda Skocpol's *States and Social Revolutions*
Adam Smith's *The Wealth of Nations*
Timothy Snyder's *Bloodlands: Europe Between Hitler and Stalin*
Sun Tzu's *The Art of War*
Keith Thomas's *Religion and the Decline of Magic*
Thucydides's *The History of the Peloponnesian War*
Frederick Jackson Turner's *The Significance of the Frontier in American History*
Odd Arne Westad's *The Global Cold War: Third World Interventions And The Making Of Our Times*

LITERATURE

Chinua Achebe's *An Image of Africa: Racism in Conrad's Heart of Darkness*
Roland Barthes's *Mythologies*
Homi K. Bhabha's *The Location of Culture*
Judith Butler's *Gender Trouble*
Simone De Beauvoir's *The Second Sex*
Ferdinand De Saussure's *Course in General Linguistics*
T. S. Eliot's *The Sacred Wood: Essays on Poetry and Criticism*
Zora Neale Huston's *Characteristics of Negro Expression*
Toni Morrison's *Playing in the Dark: Whiteness in the American Literary Imagination*
Edward Said's *Orientalism*
Gayatri Chakravorty Spivak's *Can the Subaltern Speak?*
Mary Wollstonecraft's *A Vindication of the Rights of Women*
Virginia Woolf's *A Room of One's Own*

PHILOSOPHY

Elizabeth Anscombe's *Modern Moral Philosophy*
Hannah Arendt's *The Human Condition*
Aristotle's *Metaphysics*
Aristotle's *Nicomachean Ethics*
Edmund Gettier's *Is Justified True Belief Knowledge?*
Georg Wilhelm Friedrich Hegel's *Phenomenology of Spirit*
David Hume's *Dialogues Concerning Natural Religion*
David Hume's *The Enquiry for Human Understanding*
Immanuel Kant's *Religion within the Boundaries of Mere Reason*
Immanuel Kant's *Critique of Pure Reason*
Søren Kierkegaard's *The Sickness Unto Death*
Søren Kierkegaard's *Fear and Trembling*
C. S. Lewis's *The Abolition of Man*
Alasdair MacIntyre's *After Virtue*
Marcus Aurelius's *Meditations*
Friedrich Nietzsche's *On the Genealogy of Morality*
Friedrich Nietzsche's *Beyond Good and Evil*
Plato's *Republic*
Plato's *Symposium*
Jean-Jacques Rousseau's *The Social Contract*
Gilbert Ryle's *The Concept of Mind*
Baruch Spinoza's *Ethics*
Sun Tzu's *The Art of War*
Ludwig Wittgenstein's *Philosophical Investigations*

POLITICS

Benedict Anderson's *Imagined Communities*
Aristotle's *Politics*
Bernard Bailyn's *The Ideological Origins of the American Revolution*
Edmund Burke's *Reflections on the Revolution in France*
John C. Calhoun's *A Disquisition on Government*
Ha-Joon Chang's *Kicking Away the Ladder*
Hamid Dabashi's *Iran: A People Interrupted*
Hamid Dabashi's *Theology of Discontent: The Ideological Foundation of the Islamic Revolution in Iran*
Robert Dahl's *Democracy and its Critics*
Robert Dahl's *Who Governs?*
David Brion Davis's *The Problem of Slavery in the Age of Revolution*

Alexis De Tocqueville's *Democracy in America*
James Ferguson's *The Anti-Politics Machine*
Frank Dikotter's *Mao's Great Famine*
Sheila Fitzpatrick's *Everyday Stalinism*
Eric Foner's *Reconstruction: America's Unfinished Revolution, 1863-1877*
Milton Friedman's *Capitalism and Freedom*
Francis Fukuyama's *The End of History and the Last Man*
John Lewis Gaddis's *We Now Know: Rethinking Cold War History*
Ernest Gellner's *Nations and Nationalism*
David Graeber's *Debt: the First 5000 Years*
Antonio Gramsci's *The Prison Notebooks*
Alexander Hamilton, John Jay & James Madison's *The Federalist Papers*
Friedrich Hayek's *The Road to Serfdom*
Christopher Hill's *The World Turned Upside Down*
Thomas Hobbes's *Leviathan*
John A. Hobson's *Imperialism: A Study*
Samuel P. Huntington's *The Clash of Civilizations and the Remaking of World Order*
Tony Judt's *Postwar: A History of Europe Since 1945*
David C. Kang's *China Rising: Peace, Power and Order in East Asia*
Paul Kennedy's *The Rise and Fall of Great Powers*
Robert Keohane's *After Hegemony*
Martin Luther King Jr.'s *Why We Can't Wait*
Henry Kissinger's *World Order: Reflections on the Character of Nations and the Course of History*
John Locke's *Two Treatises of Government*
Niccolò Machiavelli's *The Prince*
Thomas Robert Malthus's *An Essay on the Principle of Population*
Mahmood Mamdani's *Citizen and Subject: Contemporary Africa And The Legacy Of Late Colonialism*
Karl Marx's *Capital*
John Stuart Mill's *On Liberty*
John Stuart Mill's *Utilitarianism*
Hans Morgenthau's *Politics Among Nations*
Thomas Paine's *Common Sense*
Thomas Paine's *Rights of Man*
Thomas Piketty's *Capital in the Twenty-First Century*
Robert D. Putman's *Bowling Alone*
John Rawls's *Theory of Justice*
Jean-Jacques Rousseau's *The Social Contract*
Theda Skocpol's *States and Social Revolutions*
Adam Smith's *The Wealth of Nations*
Sun Tzu's *The Art of War*
Henry David Thoreau's *Civil Disobedience*
Thucydides's *The History of the Peloponnesian War*
Kenneth Waltz's *Theory of International Politics*
Max Weber's *Politics as a Vocation*
Odd Arne Westad's *The Global Cold War: Third World Interventions And The Making Of Our Times*

POSTCOLONIAL STUDIES

Roland Barthes's *Mythologies*
Frantz Fanon's *Black Skin, White Masks*
Homi K. Bhabha's *The Location of Culture*
Gustavo Gutiérrez's *A Theology of Liberation*
Edward Said's *Orientalism*
Gayatri Chakravorty Spivak's *Can the Subaltern Speak?*

PSYCHOLOGY

Gordon Allport's *The Nature of Prejudice*
Alan Baddeley & Graham Hitch's *Aggression: A Social Learning Analysis*
Albert Bandura's *Aggression: A Social Learning Analysis*
Leon Festinger's *A Theory of Cognitive Dissonance*
Sigmund Freud's *The Interpretation of Dreams*
Betty Friedan's *The Feminine Mystique*
Michael R. Gottfredson & Travis Hirschi's *A General Theory of Crime*
Eric Hoffer's *The True Believer: Thoughts on the Nature of Mass Movements*
William James's *Principles of Psychology*
Elizabeth Loftus's *Eyewitness Testimony*
A. H. Maslow's *A Theory of Human Motivation*
Stanley Milgram's *Obedience to Authority*
Steven Pinker's *The Better Angels of Our Nature*
Oliver Sacks's *The Man Who Mistook His Wife For a Hat*
Richard Thaler & Cass Sunstein's *Nudge: Improving Decisions About Health, Wealth and Happiness*
Amos Tversky's *Judgment under Uncertainty: Heuristics and Biases*
Philip Zimbardo's *The Lucifer Effect*

SCIENCE

Rachel Carson's *Silent Spring*
William Cronon's *Nature's Metropolis: Chicago And The Great West*
Alfred W. Crosby's *The Columbian Exchange*
Charles Darwin's *On the Origin of Species*
Richard Dawkin's *The Selfish Gene*
Thomas Kuhn's *The Structure of Scientific Revolutions*
Geoffrey Parker's *Global Crisis: War, Climate Change and Catastrophe in the Seventeenth Century*
Mathis Wackernagel & William Rees's *Our Ecological Footprint*

SOCIOLOGY

Michelle Alexander's *The New Jim Crow: Mass Incarceration in the Age of Colorblindness*
Gordon Allport's *The Nature of Prejudice*
Albert Bandura's *Aggression: A Social Learning Analysis*
Hanna Batatu's *The Old Social Classes And The Revolutionary Movements Of Iraq*
Ha-Joon Chang's *Kicking Away the Ladder*
W. E. B. Du Bois's *The Souls of Black Folk*
Émile Durkheim's *On Suicide*
Frantz Fanon's *Black Skin, White Masks*
Frantz Fanon's *The Wretched of the Earth*
Eric Foner's *Reconstruction: America's Unfinished Revolution, 1863-1877*
Eugene Genovese's *Roll, Jordan, Roll: The World the Slaves Made*
Jack Goldstone's *Revolution and Rebellion in the Early Modern World*
Antonio Gramsci's *The Prison Notebooks*
Richard Herrnstein & Charles A Murray's *The Bell Curve: Intelligence and Class Structure in American Life*
Eric Hoffer's *The True Believer: Thoughts on the Nature of Mass Movements*
Jane Jacobs's *The Death and Life of Great American Cities*
Robert Lucas's *Why Doesn't Capital Flow from Rich to Poor Countries?*
Jay Macleod's *Ain't No Makin' It: Aspirations and Attainment in a Low Income Neighborhood*
Elaine May's *Homeward Bound: American Families in the Cold War Era*
Douglas McGregor's *The Human Side of Enterprise*
C. Wright Mills's *The Sociological Imagination*

Thomas Piketty's *Capital in the Twenty-First Century*
Robert D. Putman's *Bowling Alone*
David Riesman's *The Lonely Crowd: A Study of the Changing American Character*
Edward Said's *Orientalism*
Joan Wallach Scott's *Gender and the Politics of History*
Theda Skocpol's *States and Social Revolutions*
Max Weber's *The Protestant Ethic and the Spirit of Capitalism*

THEOLOGY

Augustine's *Confessions*
Benedict's *Rule of St Benedict*
Gustavo Gutiérrez's *A Theology of Liberation*
Carole Hillenbrand's *The Crusades: Islamic Perspectives*
David Hume's *Dialogues Concerning Natural Religion*
Immanuel Kant's *Religion within the Boundaries of Mere Reason*
Ernst Kantorowicz's *The King's Two Bodies: A Study in Medieval Political Theology*
Søren Kierkegaard's *The Sickness Unto Death*
C. S. Lewis's *The Abolition of Man*
Saba Mahmood's *The Politics of Piety: The Islamic Revival and the Feminist Subject*
Baruch Spinoza's *Ethics*
Keith Thomas's *Religion and the Decline of Magic*

COMING SOON

Chris Argyris's *The Individual and the Organisation*
Seyla Benhabib's *The Rights of Others*
Walter Benjamin's *The Work Of Art in the Age of Mechanical Reproduction*
John Berger's *Ways of Seeing*
Pierre Bourdieu's *Outline of a Theory of Practice*
Mary Douglas's *Purity and Danger*
Roland Dworkin's *Taking Rights Seriously*
James G. March's *Exploration and Exploitation in Organisational Learning*
Ikujiro Nonaka's *A Dynamic Theory of Organizational Knowledge Creation*
Griselda Pollock's *Vision and Difference*
Amartya Sen's *Inequality Re-Examined*
Susan Sontag's *On Photography*
Yasser Tabbaa's *The Transformation of Islamic Art*
Ludwig von Mises's *Theory of Money and Credit*

Macat Disciplines

Access the greatest ideas and thinkers across entire disciplines, including

Postcolonial Studies

Roland Barthes's *Mythologies*
Frantz Fanon's *Black Skin, White Masks*
Homi K. Bhabha's *The Location of Culture*
Gustavo Gutiérrez's *A Theology of Liberation*
Edward Said's *Orientalism*
Gayatri Chakravorty Spivak's *Can the Subaltern Speak?*

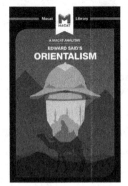

Macat analyses are available from all good bookshops and libraries.

Access hundreds of analyses through one, multimedia tool.
Join free for one month **library.macat.com**

Macat Disciplines

Access the greatest ideas and thinkers across entire disciplines, including

AFRICANA STUDIES

Chinua Achebe's *An Image of Africa: Racism in Conrad's Heart of Darkness*

W. E. B. Du Bois's *The Souls of Black Folk*

Zora Neale Hurston's *Characteristics of Negro Expression*

Martin Luther King Jr.'s *Why We Can't Wait*

Toni Morrison's *Playing in the Dark: Whiteness in the American Literary Imagination*

Macat analyses are available from all good bookshops and libraries.

Access hundreds of analyses through one, multimedia tool.
Join free for one month **library.macat.com**

Macat Disciplines

Access the greatest ideas and thinkers across entire disciplines, including

FEMINISM, GENDER AND QUEER STUDIES

Simone De Beauvoir's
The Second Sex

Michel Foucault's
History of Sexuality

Betty Friedan's
The Feminine Mystique

Saba Mahmood's
*The Politics of Piety:
The Islamic Revival and
the Feminist Subject*

Joan Wallach Scott's
*Gender and the
Politics of History*

Mary Wollstonecraft's
*A Vindication of the
Rights of Woman*

Virginia Woolf's
A Room of One's Own

Judith Butler's
Gender Trouble

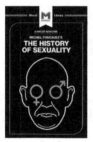

Macat Disciplines

Access the greatest ideas and thinkers across entire disciplines, including

CRIMINOLOGY

Michelle Alexander's
*The New Jim Crow:
Mass Incarceration in the
Age of Colorblindness*

**Michael R. Gottfredson
& Travis Hirschi's**
A General Theory of Crime

Elizabeth Loftus's
Eyewitness Testimony

**Richard Herrnstein
& Charles A. Murray's**
*The Bell Curve: Intelligence and
Class Structure in American Life*

Jay Macleod's
*Ain't No Makin' It:
Aspirations and Attainment in a
Low-Income Neighborhood*

Philip Zimbardo's
The Lucifer Effect

Macat analyses are available from all good bookshops and libraries.

Access hundreds of analyses through one, multimedia tool.
Join free for one month **library.macat.com**

Macat Disciplines

Access the greatest ideas and thinkers across entire disciplines, including

INEQUALITY

Ha-Joon Chang's, *Kicking Away the Ladder*

David Graeber's, *Debt: The First 5000 Years*

Robert E. Lucas's, *Why Doesn't Capital Flow from Rich To Poor Countries?*

Thomas Piketty's, *Capital in the Twenty-First Century*

Amartya Sen's, *Inequality Re-Examined*

Mahbub Ul Haq's, *Reflections on Human Development*

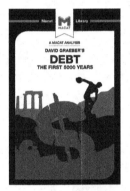

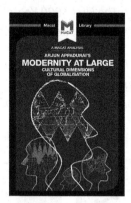

Macat Disciplines

Access the greatest ideas and thinkers across entire disciplines, including

MAN AND THE ENVIRONMENT

The Brundtland Report's, *Our Common Future*
Rachel Carson's, *Silent Spring*
James Lovelock's, *Gaia: A New Look at Life on Earth*
Mathis Wackernagel & William Rees's, *Our Ecological Footprint*

Macat analyses are available from all good bookshops and libraries.

Access hundreds of analyses through one, multimedia tool.
Join free for one month **library.macat.com**

Macat Disciplines

Access the greatest ideas and thinkers across entire disciplines, including

THE FUTURE OF DEMOCRACY

Robert A. Dahl's, *Democracy and Its Critics*
Robert A. Dahl's, *Who Governs?*
Alexis De Toqueville's, *Democracy in America*
Niccolò Machiavelli's, *The Prince*
John Stuart Mill's, *On Liberty*
Robert D. Putnam's, *Bowling Alone*
Jean-Jacques Rousseau's, *The Social Contract*
Henry David Thoreau's, *Civil Disobedience*

Macat Disciplines

Access the greatest ideas and thinkers across entire disciplines, including

TOTALITARIANISM

Sheila Fitzpatrick's, *Everyday Stalinism*
Ian Kershaw's, *The "Hitler Myth"*
Timothy Snyder's, *Bloodlands*